Business Hints for Men and Women

A. R. Calhoun

CHAPTER I

COMMON SENSE FARMING

The three things essential to all wealth production are land, labor, and capital.

"The dry land" was created before there appeared the man, the laborer, to work it. With his bare hands the worker could have done nothing with the land either as a grazer, a farmer or a miner. From the very first he needed capital, that is, the tools to work the land.

The first tool may have been a pole, one end hardened in the fire, or a combined hoe and axe, made by fastening with wythes, a suitable stone to the end of a stick; but no matter the kind of tool, or the means of producing it, it represented capital, and the man who owned this tool was a capitalist as compared with the man without any such appliance.

From the land, with the aid of labor and capital, comes wealth, which in a broad way may be defined as something having an exchangeable value.

Before the appearance of money all wealth changed hands through barter. The wealth in the world to-day is immeasurably greater than all the money in it. The business of the world, particularly between nations, is still carried on through exchange, the balances being settled by money.

Money is a medium of exchange, and should not be confounded with wealth or capital; the latter is that form of wealth which is used with labor in all production.

Broadly speaking, wealth is of two kinds, dormant and active. The former awaits the development of labor and capital, the latter is the product of both.

Labor is human effort, in any form, used for the production of wealth. It is of two kinds—skilled and unskilled. The former may be wholly mental, the latter may be wholly manual.

The successful farmer must be a skilled laborer, no matter the amount of his manual work. The unskilled farmer can never succeed largely, no matter how hard he works.

Trained hands with trained brains are irresistible.

Too many farmers live in the ruts cut by their great-great- grandfathers. They still balance the corn in the sack with a stone.

Farming is the world's greatest industry. All the ships might be docked, all the factory wheels stopped, and all the railroads turned to streaks of rust, and still the race would survive, but let the plow lie idle for a year and man would perish as when the deluge swept the mountain tops.

The next census will show considerably over 6,000,000 farms in the United States. Farming is the greatest of all industries, as it is the most essential. Our Government has wisely made the head of the Department of Agriculture a cabinet officer, and the effect on our farming interest is shown in improved methods and a larger output of better quality.

The hap-hazard, unskilled methods of the past are disappearing. Science is lending her aid to the tiller of the soil, and the wise ones are reaching out their hands in welcome.

BUSINESS METHODS NEEDED

As farming is our principal business, it follows that those who conduct this vast and varied enterprise should be business men.

The farmer is a producer of goods, and so might be regarded as a manufacturer,—the original meaning of the word is one who makes things by hand. He is also a seller of his own products, and a purchaser of the products of others, so that, to some extent, he may also be regarded as a trader or merchant.

Enterprise and business skill are the requisites of the manufacturer and merchant. Can the farmer succeed without them?

No business can prosper without method, economy, and industry intelligently applied.

No man works harder the year round than does the American farmer, yet too many are going back instead of advancing. In such cases it will be found that there is enough hard work for better results, and that the cause of failure is that the industry has not been properly applied, and that economy has had no consideration.

Economy does not mean niggardliness, or a determination to get along without tools that your neighbor has purchased. A neglect to secure the best tool needed might be classed as an extravagance, a waste, if the tool in question could have added to the quality and quantity of the output, without the expenditure of more labor.

Business common-sense is taking the place of old-fashioned conservatism and scientific methods are no longer sneered at as "book-farming."

CHAPTER II

DOCUMENTS EVERY FARMER SHOULD UNDERSTAND

All property implies an owner. Property is of two kinds, real and personal. The former is permanent and fixed, the latter can be moved.

Every occupant of realty holds it through a deed, which carries with it sole ownership, or through a lease which carries with it the right to occupation and use in accordance with the conditions as to time and the amount to be paid, set forth in the written instrument.

A deed carries with it sole ownership, a lease covers the right of use for a fixed period.

AS TO DEEDS

The purchaser of real estate, say a farm, should receive, from the person selling the property, a written instrument, or conveyance known as a deed.

The deed must show clearly that the title to or interest in the property has been transferred from the seller to the buyer.

Before the deed is signed and delivered, the buyer should know that he is getting a clear title to the property described in the conveyance.

In order to insure the accuracy of the title and thus avoid subsequent complications and perhaps lawsuits, the paper should be submitted to some good lawyer, or other person acquainted with real estate law and the methods by which titles are traced from the first owner to the present possessor.

TITLE ABSTRACTS

In all the great business centers of the United States there are Title Guarantee Companies, who for a consideration—to be paid by the seller— furnish an abstract of title, and insure its validity.

In smaller places the local lawyers know how to make up an abstract and one should be employed. Never trust the search of the inexperienced.

An abstract of title is a memorandum taken from the records of the office where deeds are recorded, and showing the history of the title from the Government up to the present time.

The seller should furnish the buyer with a certificate from the proper county officer, showing whether or not all taxes have been paid up to the last assessment.

In addition to this, before the money is paid and the deed accepted, the purchaser should be satisfied that there are no mortgages, liens, attachments or other claims against the property.

If such claims exist and are known to the buyer, he may assume them as a condition of the sale.

PARTIES TO A DEED

The person selling the land and making the deed is known in law as the Grantor. The person buying the property is known as the Grantee.

A deed is a form of contract, and in order to have its terms and statements binding on the maker, he must be twenty-one years of age, or over, and he must be of sound mind.

The grantee need not be twenty-one, nor of sound mind in order to make the terms of the deed binding on the grantor.

In some states, if the grantor be a married man, his wife must sign the deed with him. This should be seen to, for without the wife's signature the grantee will not have a clear title, for the woman could still claim an interest in the property equal to her dower right.

Also, if the grantor is a woman, her husband, for the reasons given, should join with her in the execution of the deed.

The preparation of a deed should not be left to the unskilled.

DIFFERENT DEEDS

There are three kinds of deeds, viz.: General warranty deeds, special warranty deeds, and quit-claim deeds.

The general warranty deed, if it can be had, is the one every purchaser should get.

In the general warranty deed the grantor agrees for himself, "his heirs, executors, administrators, and assigns," that at the time of making the deed he is lawfully in possession, "seized" is the legal term, of the estate described in the deed, that it is free from all incumbrance, and that he will warrant and defend the grantee and his heirs and assigns against all claims whatsoever.

In the quit-claim deed the grantor conveys to the purchaser his interest in or right to the property under consideration.

The quit-claim grantor does not guarantee the title to the property, nor warrant the grantee against any other claims. He simply, by the deed, quits his claim to the property.

The special warranty deed covenants and warrants only against the acts of the grantor and those claiming title under him.

MAKING A DEED

After a deed is properly drawn, it is ready to be signed, sealed, and delivered to the grantee.

If the wife of the grantor is to sign, her name should follow that of her husband.

If one or both cannot write, the signature can be made in this way:

His

George X Jones.

Mark.

Witness..............

In some states one or more witnesses are required to the signature of the grantor; in others, witnesses are not necessary, except where a "mark" is made.

An important part of a deed is the Acknowledgment. This is the act of acknowledging before a notary public, justice or other official properly qualified to administer an oath, that the signatures are genuine and made voluntarily.

The acknowledgment having been taken, the official stamps the paper with his seal and signs it.

In some states the law requires that a wax or paper seal be attached to the paper, while in others a circular scroll, made with the pen, with the letters "L.S." in the center answer the purpose.

When the foregoing essentials are complied with the deed must be delivered to the grantee. The delivery is essential, for without it the deed is of no value, even though every other requisite be complied with.

A deed may be made for land on which full payment has already been acknowledged, but if the grantor dies before the deed is delivered, then the deed has no legal value.

A deed obtained by fraud, deceit or compulsion is void.

RECORDING DEEDS

As soon as possible after the grantee has received the deed, he should have it recorded.

In every county in the different states there is an officer, known as register or recorder, whose duty it is to enter in regular folios, or books, a copy of every deed or mortgage presented to him. The document then becomes a part of the county records.

The grantee must pay the recording fees.

Anyone, on paying the fee for copying and certifying, can obtain a copy of any document that has been recorded in a register's office.

If an original deed is lost, the certified copy of the register has all the legality of the original.

All deeds and other papers of value should be carefully kept, so that they may be available, if needed.

A small safe deposit box with a company that keeps such spaces for rent, is often a wise investment.

Keep all related papers in one package or envelope.

If there is one lawyer who attends to all your legal business, he will be a good custodian of all papers of record, for he usually has a fireproof safe.

CHAPTER III

OTHER FORMS OF DEEDS—MORTGAGES

There is one condition under which the grantor does not turn over or deliver the deed to the grantee after it is made. This is known as a Deed in Escrow.

A deed "delivered in escrow" is when the document is placed with a third party to be by him delivered to the grantee when a certain time has elapsed or certain conditions have been fulfilled.

When the conditions have been complied with, the deed is given by its custodian to the grantee, which is as legal as if it were given by the grantor in person.

TRUST DEEDS

A trust deed is the form used to convey property to some person who is entitled to its proceeds or profits.

This form of deed is often used to secure the payment of a debt.

In some states they take the place of mortgages.

Where the trust deed is meant to take the place of a mortgage to secure a debt payment, the property is deeded to a third party known as a "trustee."

The trustee in this case is the agent for debtor and creditor, and he must act impartially.

The trust deed specifies the character of the debt to be secured. In case of failure to pay the debt as agreed on, the trustee may, if so warranted, sell the property, and pay the obligation from the proceeds.

The grantor in a trust deed, if not stipulated to the contrary, is entitled to all the rents and profits of the property; for it remains virtually his, until he has failed to fill his contract.

When the indebtedness secured by the trust deed has been paid, the trustee must at once execute a paper known to law as a Release Deed. When recorded this instrument discharges the lien.

AS TO MORTGAGES

Mortgages are of two kinds, real and chattel. The first is a lien on real estate, the second on personal property.

A mortgage may be defined as a conveyance of property, personal or real, as security for the payment of a debt, or it may be given as a guarantee for the performance of some particular duty.

MORTGAGE FORMS

When a mortgage is given as security for the payment of a debt, the rule is to give a note for the payment of the amount involved. The mortgage becomes in this case the security for the note's payment.

In the body of the note it must be stated that it is secured by mortgage.

The date of the note and mortgage should be the same.

The man who mortgages his property is the mortgagor.

The man to whom the mortgage is given is the mortgagee.

The form of the mortgage is the same as that of a deed, except that it contains a clause called the Defeasance, which states that when the obligation has been met the document shall be void.

MORTGAGES MUST BE RECORDED

The forms for "signing, sealing and delivering" a mortgage, are the same as with a deed.

A mortgage must be recorded the same as a deed, the mortgagee paying the fees.

Chattel mortgages are filed and recorded in the same way, except that it is not usual to make copies of the instrument. They are described in books prepared for the purpose.

A wife need not join her husband in making the note secured by a mortgage, but if she agrees to the transaction it is necessary for her to sign the mortgage; however, some states do not require this.

PAYMENTS

Often a life insurance policy is used as security for the payment of a mortgage.

The mortgagee, if there be buildings on the property, should see that the buildings are insured and that the policy or policies are made out in his name.

If the insurance policy is in the mortgagor's name he may collect and keep the insurance money.

The mortgagor must meet, as stipulated, every payment of the principal and interest.

Failure to meet one payment can result in a legal foreclosure.

When a payment is made, the date and the amount must be entered on the back of the note. This should be done in the presence of the mortgagor.

If possible always pay the obligation by check.

If a payment is accepted on a mortgage and the amount is not sufficient to meet the sum required, the interest is first settled in full, the rest is credited to the principal.

When the full amount, with interest, is paid in, it becomes the duty of the mortgagee to have the mortgage "discharged."

A complete settlement is when, all payments being made, the mortgagee surrenders the note and its security, and causes to be written by the register, on the margin of the copy in his books, the words, "discharged," or "satisfied," affixing thereto his official signature and the date.

ASSIGNMENTS

A mortgage is regarded in law as personal property.

A mortgage need not remain in the hands of the mortgagee in order to be valid. It can be sold like bonds, stocks or other property, and there are men who deal only in that form of security.

In order to sell a mortgage, the owner must make, to the purchaser, what is known as an "assignment of mortgage."

The assignment should be recorded in the same way as the original mortgage, the assignee paying the fee.

REDEMPTION OF MORTGAGES

While the rule as to the redemption of mortgages remains the same in some localities that it formerly was, the law in most places is now more lenient.

Now the mortgagor who has failed is usually given by law an extension of time in which to make good the payment of principal and interest.

Lenders, when the interest is met, are content to let the mortgage run on as an investment, though it will often be found, in such cases, that it is better to make a new mortgage.

EQUITY OF REDEMPTION

Where the payments on a mortgage have not been met and the instrument has not been foreclosed, the mortgagor has still what is known as an "equity of redemption."

In some states after the foreclosure of the mortgage and the sale of the property there is still a period of redemption of from sixty days to six years.

The mode of foreclosure differs in some states. The usual method is to foreclose on an order from the court, and to have the sale conducted by a court officer.

The proceeds from the sale are used to pay the principal, interests and costs. If there is money left over it is paid to the mortgagor, whose interests in the property are then at an end.

Many people, not familiar with business methods, are inclined to regard a mortgage as something of a disgrace, when, as a matter of fact it is a most usual and honorable means of raising money for the securing of a home or the conducting of a business.

Nearly all of the great railroads of the country have been built by the sale of the mortgage bonds, which are usually renewed when due, and are sought out as a safe and sane form of investment.

The fact that a mortgage payment has to be met on a farm is often in itself the strongest inducement to industry and economy.

CHAPTER IV

WILLS

Whether farmer, manufacturer, merchant or professional man, and whether in youth, mid-age or declining years, every owner of personal or real property, or both, should make a will.

If you have not made a will, get over the foolish notion that it is a premonition of death, and do so at once.

A will is a written and signed declaration of the disposition one wishes to have made of his property in the event of his death.

The maker of a valid will must be of sound mind and not less than twenty-one years of age.

Women, whether married or single, if of proper age, are competent to make a will.

OF TWO KINDS

A will may be written or unwritten.

Unwritten wills are known as "nun-cupative." Nun-cupative wills are employed only when through accident, or sudden seizure by a fatal disease, the time necessary to write and sign a will cannot be had.

The unwritten will must be authenticated by reliable and unprejudiced witnesses, and generally it can dispose of personal property only.

In the written will no precise form is necessary, though when drawn by a lawyer it usually begins with some such form as: "I, George Brown, being of sound mind and good understanding, do make and declare this to be my last will and testament", etc.

A will is not necessarily permanent. It may be cancelled or changed in any way by the maker before his death, or a new will can be made.

The last will cancels all preceding wills.

An addition to an existing will is known as a "codicil."

A man making a will is called a testator.

A woman making a will is called a testatrix.

LIMITATIONS OF WILLS

A man has a right to dispose of his property by will or gift as he chooses, but if he is married the law compels him to consider the rights of another.

The husband cannot, by will or otherwise, deprive his wife of her "right of dower" in his real estate and appurtenances.

Unless she chooses to accept, the wife need not accept other property that is bequeathed her in lieu of dower.

The wife's dower interest in her husband's estate is a life interest only. On her death it goes to the husband's heirs, as if there had been no widow.

In some states there is no right of dower.

HOW TO MAKE A WILL

The will not only shows the purpose of the testator, but it serves as a bar to litigation among the natural heirs.

Any man or woman can write out his or her will, but unless quite familiar with such work it is better to employ a lawyer for the purpose.

The person named in the will to carry out the purpose of the testator is known as the "executor".

No person, not twenty-one at the time the will is proved can act as an executor.

Neither a convict, an imbecile, nor one known to be a drug fiend or an habitual drunkard, is eligible for the post of an executor. If an executor be appointed against his will, the law does not compel him to serve.

There must be at least two witnesses to a will, some states require three.

The witnesses need not know the contents of the will, but they must understand before signing that it is a will, and they must see it signed by the testator.

Under the common law the will is void if the witnesses are beneficiaries.

In some states a will so witnessed is valid, except that the witnesses cannot receive their legacies.

All the witnesses should sign at the same time and add their addresses.

If an heir at law, say a child, is not mentioned in the will, the law assumes that he was forgotten by the testator and generally gives the share the heir would be entitled to if there were no will.

At the end of the will the testator, in the presence of the witnesses, should write his name in full.

AN EXECUTOR'S DUTIES

An executor is the legal representative of the testator. It is his duty to see that the provisions of the will are carried out.

No man is qualified to act as executor who is not competent to make a will. Executors, unless relieved by the provisions of the will, are required to file bonds, proportioned to the value of the estate, for the faithful performance of their duties.

Should there be no executor named in the will, or if the person so named refuses to act, or if he dies or resigns, the court will appoint a person to act in his place.

The executor appointed by the court is known or called an "administrator with the will annexed."

In some states the court having jurisdiction of wills and estates of deceased is known as "the probate," in others it is called the "Surrogate's Court," and in still others, "The Orphan's."

ADMINISTRATORS AND THEIR DUTIES

If a man, owning property, dies without making a will, the judge of the proper court will appoint an administrator to settle the estate.

This is the method of procedure:

1. A person, interested in getting the estate settled, goes before the proper judge and asks him to appoint an administrator. 2. The administrator must give the same bond as an executor. Their duties are the same. 3. In settling the estate the administrator is governed by the law, and by the special

directions of the officer having jurisdiction in such matters. 4. He must make a careful list of all the property belonging to the estate. The value of the personal property is estimated by men specially appointed by the court for the purpose and known as "appraisers". 5. The administrator must account for every item of property that comes into his possession. 6. All debts of deceased must be first paid, including funeral expenses. If the proceeds of the personal property are not sufficient for this purpose, the administrator may, if there be real estate, sell the whole or part of it, on an order from the court.

DEBTS

Debts must be paid in an order prescribed by law. The following is the usual order:

1. Funeral expenses and expenses of last illness. 2. The widow's allowance or award. 3. Debts due the state or municipality. 4. Claims of other creditors.

Whatever property is left, after paying these obligatory sums, is divided among the rightful heirs under the direction of the court, and in the manner provided by law.

The administrator must advertise, in one or more county papers the fact that he has been appointed to settle the estate of the deceased, whose name is given, and he must ask that all claims be presented within a given period, usually fixed at six months.

When the estate is settled to the satisfaction of the court, the same authority releases the administrator and his bondsmen.

All the fees connected with the settlement are regarded as debts and must be paid from the proceeds of the estate before closing.

THE FINAL SETTLEMENT

When the debts are paid and the residue divided among the heirs, the administrator files his account. If it is allowed the case ends.

The parties of interest in an estate may agree to settle it out of court. This saves expense, but it is not the safest way.

CHAPTER V

LETTER WRITING

What has been said about deeds and mortgages applies not only to the farmer, but also to every owner of a building lot. The same may be said of wills. They have a business interest for the town as well as for the country dweller.

BUSINESS LETTERS

The purpose of this book being "strictly business," no attempt will be made to instruct the reader in anything not connected with the subject under consideration.

Social, friendly, and such letters are matters for individual time and taste, and no rule can be laid down for their writing, but the business letter is a different matter, and one which deserves special consideration from every man or woman who receives an order by mail, or who sends one.

To write a good business letter is no mean accomplishment, and although a gift with some, it can be acquired by all.

A letter is, in a way, a testimonial of the character and ability of the writer.

The purpose of a business letter is to express just what you want and no more.

Any man with a good common school education, and a little patient practice, can soon learn to write as good a business letter as the college graduate.

Correct spelling may not be general, but it is certainly desirable.

Letter writing, as in the preparation of other papers, has its own well-recognized forms, and these may be easily learned.

Every properly constructed business letter should consist of the following parts:

1. Where written from. 2. When written. 3. To whom written. 4. Address. 5. Salutation. 6. Introduction. 7. Purpose of letter. 8. Complimentary ending. 9. Signature.

THE HEADING

The letter should begin by giving the address of the writer, followed by the date on which it was written. This will enable the recipient to direct his reply.

If from a city, the street and number should be given.

If many letters are written it will be convenient to have the permanent address of the writer printed.

The writing should be plain, and there should be no doubt in the mind of the reader as to the proper spelling of the address and signature.

Avoid the hieroglyphics which some vain men adopt in signing their names. It may be fanciful, but it does not imply consideration for the time and patience of strangers.

The following forms will serve to illustrate the type of heading used in ordinary business letters:

1

124 Smith St., Brownsville, Mass.

September 4, 1910.

Mr. John Smith,

Doylestown, Penna.

Dear Sir:

2

Leroy, Mass.,

September 5, 1910.

Messrs. Brown and Jones,

Denver, Col.

Gentlemen:

3

4 Seminole St., Fort Smith, Ark.

September 6, 1910.

Mrs. Mary J. Robinson,

Lansing, Cal.

Dear Madam:

The "Mr.," "Mrs.," "Madam," and "Miss" are titles of courtesy and should not be omitted. The abbreviation "Esq." for Esquire is sometimes used; but the two titles Mr. and Esq. should never be used with one name, as "Mr. John Smith, Esq."

If a man is known by a military or other title, always use it, but never precede it with "Mr." nor follow it with "Esq."

Clergymen should always be addressed as "Rev.," the abbreviation for Reverend. If he is a doctor of divinity, add D.D. to the name, as "Rev. John Smith, D.D."

Medical doctors may be addressed as "Dr. John Smith," or "John

Smith, M.D."

THE GREETING

The greeting or salutation is a term of courtesy or esteem used in addressing the one to whom the letter is sent.

"Sir" is the formal greeting, and is used in addressing officials, or any strange male person. "Sirs," or "Gentlemen" may be used in the plural. "Dear Sir," or "My Dear Sir," is the usual form of greeting when a business letter is addressed to an individual.

Where the writer is acquainted with the person addressed, the usual form of greeting is "Dear Mr. Smith."

THE LETTER ITSELF

If writing in response to a letter received, the writer should begin in some such way as this:

Mr. Thomas Brown,

 Newburg, N. Y.

My Dear Sir:

 Your favor of the second inst. is just to hand. In reply permit

me to state, etc., etc.

This should be followed by the necessary statement, set forth in clear, simple words.

Be sure of yourself.

The secret of good writing is clear thinking.

ENDING THE LETTER

There is much in the proper ending of a letter. In the ordinary business letter the usual ending may be, "Yours truly," "Yours very truly," or "Yours respectfully." Other endings used in writing to business acquaintances are, "Yours sincerely," or "Very sincerely yours," or you may substitute the words "Cordially" or "Heartily" for "sincerely."

SIGNING THE LETTER

The name of the writer should be so clear and distinct as to leave no doubt as to the spelling.

The name should always be written in the same way.

If your name is George W. Brown, do not write it at one time as here given, and again as G. Washington Brown, or G. W. Brown.

Adopt one form and stick to it.

If you are writing for a firm or for another as clerk or secretary, always sign the firm name, and below it your own name preceded by the word "per," meaning "by" or "through."

THE MATERIALS

Never use scraps of paper or soiled paper to write on if better can be had. The materials of a letter affect the receiver, particularly if a stranger, just as one is affected by the garb of a stranger before he speaks.

Use a good pen and black ink.

Fold your paper so that it will fit the envelope.

Avoid blots and erasures; they indicate carelessness or unbecoming haste.

Address your letter distinctly.

Here is a good form:

Mr. George W. White,

Boston,

1101 Sioux St. Mass.

LETTERS OF INTRODUCTION

At some time or another one has to write a letter of introduction, and sometimes he has had to pay for it.

If you should give such a letter to a man to introduce him to another with whom you trade, the law has held that the introducer is responsible for any reasonable bills the introduced may contract with the receiver of the letter.

Never give a letter of introduction to a man you are not sure of.

In addressing a letter of introduction which is to be handed in person, do it in this way:

Mr. George W. Brown,

Washington, D. C.

Introducing

Mr. Henry Wilson.

This shows on its face the nature of the communication.

Here is a good form:

111 Payne Ave., Montrose, Ill.

September 27, 1910.

Mr. Norman R. Lloyd,

Chicago, Ill.

Dear Mr. Lloyd:

This will introduce my esteemed friend Mr. Thomas T. Fletcher, of this town. Mr. Fletcher contemplates opening a drug store in Chicago. Should he do so he will prove an acquisition to your City. Any favor you can render him will be much appreciated by, Yours faithfully, George W. Brown.

RECOMMENDATIONS

Every man of standing and every employer of labor is at times called on to certify to the character, or to give a testimonial to some esteemed employee who is about to seek his fortune in another place.

If you are about to hire a stranger, it adds to your confidence and to his chances if he have a testimonial as to character and fitness from his last employer, or from some man whose word you value.

The letter of recommendation is usually of a general character and not addressed to any particular. It should open in this way:

"To whom it may concern."

Follow this with your testimonial and sign it.

TITLES

The President of the United States is addressed as:

"His Excellency,"

William H. Taft,

Executive Mansion,

Washington, D. C.

Cabinet officers, Senators, Congressmen, members of the Legislature, and Mayors of cities are usually addressed as "Hon.," the abbreviation of honorable.

The title "Hon." like "Esq." is often misused. After all titles of courtesy are not obligatory, unless we regard the unwritten law of custom in such matters as binding.

The very best kind of a letter, and perhaps the hardest to write, is that in which the writer appears to be talking to us face to face.

CHAPTER VI

BILLS, RECEIPTS AND ACCOUNTS

Try to understand clearly the meaning of all the business terms you have to use.

The terms "bill" and "invoice" usually mean the same thing, that is, a "bill of sale." This applies to goods sold, or services rendered.

The merchant sends you an itemized invoice of the goods you ordered and he has shipped.

The carpenter sends you an itemized bill of the work done by your order.

Such a document should be regarded not as a "dun," but rather as a record of the contract or transaction.

In the foregoing case the merchant and the carpenter are the creditors, the recipient of the goods or work is the debtor.

BILLS FOR GOODS

In writing out a bill the date is the first thing to be considered. This should be the same in form as a business letter.

This form will serve as an illustration:

Glenwood, N. J.

October 1, 1910.

Robert Brown

To George L. White, Dr.

Sept 2. For 25 lbs. sugar, at .06 . . .$1.50

" 6. " 30 lbs. ham, at .20 . . . . 6.00

" 14. " 100 lbs. flour, at .03-1/2 . 3.50

———

Received payment, $11.00

SIGNATURE ON PAYMENT

Wholesale houses send such bills as soon as the goods are shipped or delivered, though the payment, as per agreement, is not to be made for thirty, sixty or ninety days.

Where there is a running account, that is, frequent orders, with total payments never completed, it is customary for the seller, at the beginning of a calendar month to send to the creditor a "statement." This statement does not repeat the items of the bills rendered, its purpose being to show the balance due to date.

BILLS FOR LABOR

Where a mechanic or laborer is employed by the day at a fixed wage, the length of time and dates should be given.

Richmond, Va.

November 3, 1910.

Charles M. Pratt,

To John Smith, Dr.

To 4 days, from Oct. 1st to 4th

inclusive, at $2.00.........$8.00

To 2 1/2 days, Oct. 10th, 11th

and 12th................... 5.00

To 3 days, Oct. 17th, 18th and

19th 6.00

_____

Received payment, $19.00

Signature.

This bill is just as transferable as a mortgage. If for any reason Mr. Smith should decide to sell it, say to Robert Brown, he should make the following endorsement across the back:

"In consideration of ——— dollars, the receipt of which is hereby acknowledged, I do hereby sell and assign to Robert Brown, the written account, which is justly due from the within named Charles W. Pratt, and I hereby authorize the said Robert Brown to collect the same. "John Smith." "Newburg, N. Y. November 1, 1910."

Regarded simply from a business viewpoint and without considering ethics, "Honesty is the best policy."

Bills, where possible, should be promptly paid.

Prompt payment is a guarantee of credit and credit is the heart if not the soul of business.

Never, if it can be avoided, buy goods on the installment plan.

Be sure to get a receipt for all payments you make, and be equally sure to keep the receipt where you can find it.

Examine all bills and invoices; compare them with the goods received, and no matter what your faith in the seller's care and honesty, calculate for yourself the price of each item, and be sure that the total is correct.

DISCOUNT IN TRADE

It is a business custom, when a bill is paid before it is due, to allow a discount. This may be the legal rate of interest, or any percentage agreed on in advance.

Sometimes wholesale merchants or manufacturers grant esteemed customers, in consideration of prompt payments, a discount from the regular prices. This is known as "trade discount."

We often read of two or more discounts. A store keeper buys a bill of goods for $350 and is granted 20% and 5% from the selling price.

This does not mean a discount of 25% as the uninitiated might think. The 20% is deducted from the $350, that is, $70, leaving $280. Then the 5%, $14, is deducted from this, leaving $260.

Partial payments are not endorsed on the bill. The receipt is written on a separate piece of paper. It differs from the usual receipt in that the one is "in full payment" and the other "on account."

Receipt no bill before it is actually paid.

Some one has translated the letters "C. O. D." into "Come omejitly Down." The Collect on Delivery usually accompanies goods sent by express.

FORMS OF RECEIPTS

A receipt for a partial payment:

Leavenworth, Kansas.

December 7, 1910.

$75.00

Received from Charles Long seventy-five

dollars on account.

Henry S. Somers.

A receipt in full:

San Diego, Cal.

July 27, 1910.

$260.75

Received from N. O. Taylor, two hundred

and sixty 75-100 dollars, in full payment

to date. Samuel G. Novris.

Another form:

Portland, Me.

October 20, 1910.

$40.00

Received from Thomas Moore, ten cords

of hardwood, at $4.00 a cord, the sum to

be applied to his account.

Daniel Forman.

In payment of rent:

$17.00

Received from William Forbes seventeen

dollars in full payment of rent of premises

No. 24 West Street, for the month ending

October 31, 1910.

Philip F. Ross.

Where one person pays for another:

Wilmington, Del.

August 17, 1910.

$80.00

Received from Alfred Thompson eighty

dollars to apply to the account of Hiram O.

Wells.

Baker Jones & Co.,

per, S. N. Thorp.

Receipts and other documents signed with a mark X should be witnessed.

Payment on a note:

Bridgeport, Conn.

July 1, 1910.

$150.00

Received from Casper N. Work one

hundred and fifty dollars to apply on the

payment of his note to me for six hundred

dollars, dated March 8, 1910.

Ruben Hoyt.

The maker of the note should, in addition to getting his receipt, have the amount of his payment endorsed on the back of the note by the holder.

Where a receipt is given to the administrator of an estate his position should be named as "Robert Fields, administrator of the estate of John Jones, deceased."

WHAT IS AN ORDER?

An order is a command or instruction by one person to another to do a stated thing.

An order may be given for the delivery of goods or the payment of cash.

This is the usual form:

Dayton, Ohio.

August 3, 1910.

Mr. G. W. McBride:

Please deliver to Edward Lott goods

from your store to the amount of ten dollars,

and charge to my account.

F. T. Leroy.

This would be an order for cash:

Holden, Ind.

June 18, 1910.

$30.00

Mr. P. T. Mayhew. Please pay to Thomas

Jackson thirty dollars and charge same

to my account.

F. R. Wilson.

A DUE BILL

The customary form of a due bill is:

Durham, N. C.

May 1, 1910.

$10.00

Due George Smith ten dollars, payable

in merchandise from my store.

S. T. Long.

CHAPTER VII

WHO SHOULD KEEP ACCOUNTS

To have any value, business accounts, whether of a great or a small concern, must be accurately kept.

Every man and woman, having unsettled dealings with others, should keep some sort of book accounts.

Storekeepers must keep accounts, and every farmer and mechanic, who would know just what he owns and what he has spent during the past month and year, should keep an exact account of every cent received and paid out.

Lawyers and doctors know how to keep accounts, or if they do not they are neglecting their own side of their professional duties.

Workers, skilled and unskilled, and even the hired girl who is paid by the month, should keep a record of the compensation received, and how the whole or the part has been expended.

No woman can be called a really good housekeeper who does not know to a penny what has become of the money she has received for the upkeep of her establishment, whether she have a score of servants or does all her own work.

In order to keep such accounts, as have just been indicated, it is not necessary to be a trained bookkeeper, or to know anything more about the art than a good common school education gives.

Another word as to the farmer. I am not thinking in this connection of the old-time, deep-in-the-ruts farmer, who never learns and knows nothing to forget, but of that wide-awake producer who tries to keep up with the times.

Not only should the farmer keep cash accounts, the form may be quite simple, but all his business affairs should be kept in the best possible trim.

Personal agreements without some kind of writing to back them up, are dangerous.

Verbal contracts feed the lawyers.

All transactions involving labor or money should be recorded in black and white.

Don't trust to your memory.

Don't rely on the memory of another.

AN ACCOUNT WITH CROPS

Every farmer should keep an account with each crop he raises and even with every field he cultivates.

Against the farm should be charged—

1. Its annual rental value. 2. What all the labor would cost if hired. 3. New machinery. 4. Wear, tear and repair of old machinery. 5. Taxes. 6. Insurance. 7. Doctor's bills. 8. Interest on mortgage if any. 9. The cost of fodder, fuel, etc., consumed.

The farm should be credited with—

1. The rent. 2. The cost of everything produced and consumed on place. 3. The farm products sold. 4. The stock sold. 5. Increased value of stock. 6. Increased value of property, if any.

Such accounts you say will cause trouble; well, you cannot do anything of value without trouble. The question is will the effort pay? Those who keep such accounts say it does, and they are usually the successful, progressive farmers.

WORKING-MEN'S ACCOUNTS

The working man, skilled or unskilled, and the working man's wife as well, should keep some form of cash book that will show from week to week the receipts and expenditures.

One can be thrifty without being miserly.

Where did the money go?

Look at your book, where every cent expended has been set down, and you will be surprised to find how the little sums total up.

Look over the list of little things bought and you will be surprised to see how many were not needed.

Here is a simple form for a home record:

Cash Received

1910.

Jan. 2. Balance on hand.........$45.50

" 3. Work for Mr. Jones....... 1.75

" 3. Smith paid bill......... 13.75

" 9. Work for Mr. Brown....... 7.50

Cash Paid

1910.

Jan. 2. Two shirts...............$1.50

" 3. To wife for house........ 8.50

" 4. Doctor C's. bill......... 6.00

" 5. Fare to Troy............. 2.25

" 6. Horse car................ .20

" 6. Postage.................. .06

" 7. Church Contribution...... 1.00

" 8. Shoes mended............. 0.60

" 9. Newspaper bill........... 1.00

Never "lump" what you receive or what you spend.

Set down each item separately, even to one cent.

When you have filled out each page of "received" and "paid" foot it up and carry it to the next page set apart for the purpose.

An account book will cost but a few cents. Use the left-hand side for receipts and the right for expenditures.

At any time the excess of the left hand over the right should show the amount on hand.

Strike a balance at least once a month.

OTHER RECORDS

Never mix up another's accounts with your own.

John Smith, treasurer of some church, society, or club, is a different person before the law from John Smith, the trader or mechanic.

Funds not your own, and which may be added to or decreased from time to time, as in the case of a society, say like the Odd Fellows, should be kept in the bank not as John Smith's but as the funds of "John Smith, Treasurer of Washington Lodge 110, Independent Order of Odd Fellows," or whatever the name of the society, club, or church may be.

In the same way, "a treasurer's book" should be kept and all the receipts and expenditures carefully recorded.

COPIES

If a business proposition is made to another by mail, or if you hand another in writing your proposition as to a certain contract you are willing to undertake, for the consideration named, be sure to keep a copy of the letter or contract; such a precaution may save trouble.

CHAPTER VIII

AS TO BANKS

No instrument of trade has done so much or is more essential to the safe and progressive business of the world today than the bank.

Every department of business, in our modern civilization, must keep in touch with the bank.

Money is the blood of trade and the banking system is its heart.

The bank is as necessary to the thrifty farmer as it is to the greatest railroad or the most wide-spread trust.

Banks are depositories for money not in circulation.

Banks have facilities for the safe-guarding of money which the ordinary business man could not provide for himself.

Instead of running the risk of paying bills with money carried about on his person, the business man, and every man with ready money should follow his example, deposits his money in a convenient bank, for which he receives a proper voucher in the shape of a credit in a deposit book.

When he pays a bill, he draws a check for the amount, payable to the order of his creditor. This check, when endorsed by the receiver and paid by the bank, is in itself a receipt for the money.

NATIONAL BANKS

As I propose to say something about savings banks in another chapter, the present will be devoted to what are known as "banks of deposit."

Banks of deposit are either National, State, or private.

A National bank is, as the name implies, chartered and incorporated by the Government, with special privileges and restrictions.

The Government in the organizing of National banks had in mind the protection of the public without unduly limiting the profit of the stockholders.

The sum the stockholders must contribute to the establishment of a National bank varies according to the population and the business importance of the place in which the bank is to be located.

The capital must exist in a prescribed form.

Certain forms of investment are prohibited, as for instance the ownership of real estate, except under certain restrictions.

This is done that the National bank may be able to convert its securities into cash in the shortest order.

In consideration of a prescribed amount of United States bonds, deposited with the Treasury in Washington, the Government issues to the National bank a prescribed sum in printed bank notes of varying denominations.

If the bank should close for any reason, the bank notes or their equivalent must be returned, when the bonds deposited as security are released.

Every bank must have a board of directors, a president and a cashier. Receiving and paying tellers, with bookkeepers, and many clerks are necessary to carry on the business of a large bank.

In addition, the National banks are under the supervision of regularly appointed Government inspectors.

A National bank may fail, but its notes are still "as good as gold."

BANKS AS LENDERS

The bank not only receives money on deposit, but it loans money under certain conditions.

Many merchants, builders, contractors and others often find it necessary to borrow money in order to carry on their business successfully.

If a man's business reputation is good, and the banks keep well posted in such matters, he may secure a loan on his own note, though even in such cases the name of a good endorser is required.

If in addition to his note the borrower can offer security in the way of bonds of good character, or other reliable collateral, he can usually be accommodated.

Of course, the banks charge interest for loans. They also make collections on notes and other commercial paper and they issue foreign and domestic bills of exchange.

Every man with a sum large or small in excess of his expenditures, should open a bank account. Even if not in business this will encourage thrift and lead to good business habits.

INTEREST ON DEPOSITS

Some banks, particularly those known as "state" or "private," and

National banks in smaller communities, allow interest on deposits.

This interest varies with the demand for money, but in the eastern

states it seldom goes over four per cent.

It is well to know when interest begins and ends.

If the dates set by the bank for reckoning interest are the first day of January, April, July and October, money deposited March 31st will begin to draw interest next day, but if deposited April 2nd, it would not begin to draw interest till July 1st.

But if you have the money and would insure its safety, deposit it at once regardless of time or interest.

If a depositor withdraws his money before the day when interest is due, he forfeits the interest. But banks vary as to that.

CHECK AND DEPOSIT BOOKS

Every depositor is given a book in which the teller or cashier credits him on the left-hand side with the amount deposited. Other deposits are treated in the same way, and at proper times, if interest is allowed, it is added as a deposit.

The depositor can provide his own check book, and have it printed in any color he pleases, with the name of himself and business on the margin. The bank, however, will supply loose bank checks of its own, or it may provide them in book form, with stubs, or a space on which the number, amount and purpose of the check may be noted for the drawer's information.

"Writing up" of the deposit book is leaving it with the proper officer at the bank—a receipt for the book is never taken. It is returned with all the checks received, and their amount footed up on the right hand or debit page, and the balance on hand shown.

Every depositor should know from the record on the check stubs exactly how his account stands with the bank.

Take care that you do not overdraw.

Keep your own record of your own money.

COMMERCIAL DEPOSIT BANKS

In the Commercial banks of our large cities no interest is allowed, nor could it be easily calculated where a score of deposits may be made in a week and a hundred checks drawn in a day.

The depositor in such a bank is free to check out his funds as he pleases.

Before opening an account there is more than money needed from the depositor. If unknown, he must satisfy the bank of his character, which is best done through the introduction of one known to both.

Some banks make a charge for deposits, where a man makes a convenience of them by depositing money which he checks out in a short time.

A depositor, when opening an account with a bank is required to place his signature in a book kept for the purpose. Until the bank officer, the paying teller, becomes familiar with the signature on the check, he verifies it by comparing it with that in the book.

HOW TO PREPARE A CHECK

A check may be defined to be "a written order on a bank directing it to pay a certain sum of money to the person named in the check or to his order, and signed by a depositor."

So long as the purpose is clearly conveyed in the writing no particular form of words is necessary, nor need the paper on which the check is written be the regular printed form properly filled in.

The "drawer" is the one who makes the check.

The "payee" is the one for whom the check is made.

In making a check, the best plan is to fill out the stub first, and from the data on it make out the check. This tends to accuracy.

Be sure to number your check, beginning with I.

Be sure that the number on the stub is the same as on the check.

A person having money in bank and wishing to draw for his own use, makes his check payable to "self" or to "cash."

Usual form of check:

First National Bank. No. 27

Kingston, Vt., Oct. 13, 1910.

Pay to order of John Smith

Seventy-five 75/100 ———— dollars.

$75.75 George F. Brown.

It is proper form to specify on the face of the check the purpose for which it is given, but while this is permissible it is not usual.

Write the amount of the check first in words then in figures. This makes more certain the amount.

Always begin first word of amount close to left-hand side of check; when the whole sum is written down draw a heavy stroke along the line to the word "dollars."

When a check is made payable to John Smith or order, John Smith must sign his name on the back of the check—left-hand end and about an inch from the top.

Never sign a check until you are ready to collect, or to bank it.

The payee can endorse the check to another by writing on the back as follows:

Pay to the order of

Thomas Brown.

John Smith.

A check payable to "bearer" may be negotiated by any one. When such checks are presented by a stranger, at the bank of the maker, the paying teller always insists that the stranger be identified.

Never make a check payable to "bearer" if it can be avoided.

Sometimes checks are dated ahead, for reasons satisfactory to the maker and payee.

A check drawn on August 5th, but dated August 20th cannot be collected till the latter date.

Never date a check ahead unless you are positive that you will have the money in bank to meet it on the day named.

Never, if you can avoid it in trade, receive a post-dated check.

Cash or deposit your checks as soon as possible after they are received.

If the bank should fail, while you are holding the check, the maker cannot be held for the loss.

CERTIFICATES OF DEPOSIT

Often when a depositor is travelling, he finds it convenient to carry with him a form of paper that is as good as cash, and much better in the event of loss.

Banks will issue "certified checks" to depositors. These checks are stamped by the bank "certified" with the date and officer's signature attached.

On issuing such a check, the bank debits the receiver's account with the amount, and so can guarantee the payment whenever or wherever presented.

Such a check may be received with as much certainty of its value as if it were a bank bill.

When a person places money in a bank with no intention of checking it out for some time to come, he may have issued to him a "Certificate of deposit."

While holding this certificate he cannot check against the money in the bank.

The holder of a certificate of deposit may transfer it.

The money may be paid in part by the bank, if the certificate is presented, and the amount is endorsed on the back.

To withdraw all the money the certificate must be surrendered.

USE OF CHECKS

There is no form of commercial paper in such general use as the check.

The total of all the checks in use at some seasons is far more than the total of all the money in all the banks.

Checks are balanced in the money centers through what are known as clearing houses. In these a bank is charged with checks against it and credited with those in its favor.

The differences are settled by cash.

Often a few thousand dollars will settle check accounts amounting to millions.

If by any chance you should receive a check in which your name is misspelled, or not given as you write it, endorse the check exactly as the name is written on the face, then add your name in the regular way.

CHAPTER IX

SAVINGS BANKS

While of National importance, savings banks are chartered by the respective states in which they exist, and as such are distinctly local institutions.

Unlike the National, the savings bank is not established as a money-making corporation.

The ostensible and actual purpose of the savings bank is to encourage people of small means to save.

The savings bank provides a safe place for the care of such deposits, and it pays such rates of interest on such deposits as are warranted by the earnings of its investments after paying the expenses incident to the proper conduct of its officers.

When a savings bank receives authorization to act, through a charter from the state, the organizers choose a board of directors and the proper officers.

Usually the officers occupying positions of trust and responsibility are required to give bonds for the proper discharge of their duties.

HOW BUSINESS IS CONDUCTED

With all the legal conditions complied with, and a suitable office provided, the savings bank is ready for business.

Some savings banks will receive on deposit any sum from five cents to five thousand dollars.

Other banks will not receive less than one dollar at a time, nor more than a thousand.

We have heard of "penny savings banks," but they are rarely chartered, and are organized, only to encourage thrift among children.

Fractional parts of a dollar are not usually reckoned as drawing interest.

Some banks require as much as three, four or five dollars before allowing interest.

Savings banks in the eastern states pay from three to four per cent. In the west it is sometimes as high as six.

Each bank has certain dates at which calculation of interest begins. As a rule this is January 1st, April 1st, July 1st, and October 1st.

Money deposited at any time between these dates does not draw interest till the beginning of the next quarter.

But never mind the interest.

The best time to make a deposit is when you have the money.

The bank is safer than your pocket.

HOW TO DEPOSIT

Count your money carefully and make a memorandum of the amount before giving to the savings bank to deposit.

Hand the money to the officer—usually "the receiving teller"— authorized to receive it.

The teller writes down the name, age, occupation and residence of the depositor.

If money is deposited in the name of one under legal age, the names of the parents and the birthplace of the minor are also recorded.

The adult depositor must write his name in a book provided by the bank for the signature of clients.

When these conditions are complied with, the depositor receives a memorandum book, known as a "deposit book", in which, with his name and date, is written the amount of his first deposit.

The deposit book must be carefully guarded, for without its presentation at the savings bank money cannot be drawn. You cannot check against your savings bank account, as with a commercial bank.

HOW THE ACCOUNT GROWS

After the first account is opened the rest is easy.

On the second, as on all subsequent visits, the deposit book, with the amount to be entered, is handed to the receiving teller. He counts the money, makes a record of it for his own use, enters it on your book as a deposit, and hands the book back. That is all.

Whenever interest is due it is written down in the book as if it were a cash deposit.

The interest, if desired, will be paid in cash, but if allowed to remain, it begins at once to earn interest for itself.

Interest grows like a rolling snow ball. On such small beginnings great fortunes have been built.

Savings banks keep a reserve, made up of earnings in excess of interest and all expenses.

This reserve earns money.

The money so earned is reckoned as a net profit, and it may be distributed, and usually is, among its depositors as a "dividend."

THE LIMIT OF DEPOSIT

Different banks have different limits of deposit, that is fixed sums beyond which they will not receive.

The limit is from one thousand to five thousand dollars.

When the fortunate depositor has reached the limit with one savings bank, there is no law to prevent his opening another account with another, or with any number of similar banks.

Remember the savings banks are not meant for capitalists, but for small depositors.

After deposits and interests have reached a total of $1,600, the interest will not go on earning interest, but will be regarded simply as a deposit.

This is in compliance with law.

Depositors, posted as to the law, open another account with another bank, and keep on till the interest limit is reached.

HOW TO DRAW MONEY

A savings bank depositor may either draw money himself or through some properly authorized person.

This is the method:

The deposit book is presented to the paying teller. The owner states the sum he wants to draw.

Having assured himself that the bearer of the book is the right person, the teller takes a receipt in a book kept for the purpose, for the amount, enters the same on the right hand or debit side of the book, and hands out the money.

There is a form of authorization for another to draw, printed on the deposit book. This must be copied and its directions complied with.

Most banks will not allow depositors to draw out less than a fixed sum, say $5.00.

This saves trouble, and prevents thoughtless depositors from going to the bank every time they want a dollar.

Before a depositor can draw a large sum from a savings bank he may be compelled, under the law, to give from one week to six weeks' notice of his intention.

This provision may not prevent a run on the bank, but it gives the managers time to provide for it.

Read the rules in the deposit book.

HOW SAVINGS BANKS EARN

How can a bank that does not discount notes or deal in loans and commercial paper earn money? How can it pay interest?

While they may be individually small, the aggregate of all the deposits in a savings bank may, and often do, amount to many millions.

This money is not allowed to lie idle.

Under the skilled direction of the bank officers, the money, instead of lying idle in the vaults, is invested in many ways, but always in accordance with the laws of the state under which the bank is chartered.

Much of the money is invested in mortgages on real estate, never on personal property.

National bank stocks, sound railroad bonds, and other forms of reliable interest security are fields for the investment of savings bank funds.

Savings banks are subject to the periodic inspection of state officers appointed for the purpose.

The failure of a savings bank through bad investments or the dishonesty of officials is very rare.

Avoid all banks that promise more than the regular rate of interest.

Private banks may be, and usually are, honestly conducted, but to be safe, deposit only with a bank that is regularly chartered and is subject to the inspection of the law.

The savings bank is the best for the wage earner.

CHAPTER X

NOTES—DRAFTS

The promissory note is a most useful kind of commercial paper, and it is in general use in business.

If a man has not sufficient ready cash to pay for the real estate he is about to purchase, he makes up the difference by a note, which note is secured by a mortgage on the property.

Remember the mortgage must always be regarded as security. The note represents the debt.

Often wholesalers take a note as part or even full payment for a bill of goods to a retailer.

If the wholesaler needs money, he endorses these notes and putting them in his bank draws against them, less the discount he has to pay for the accommodation.

As has been shown, an account may be transferred and sold, but a note is more convenient for that purpose.

AN ILLUSTRATION

As with a check the maker of a note is known as a "drawer," the person in whose favor it is drawn is the "payee."

Notes may be written in pencil, but it is better and safer to write with ink on good paper.

Supposing you buy a team of horses, or it may be a bill of goods, from John Brown, for $350.

Now you have only $100 in cash. What are you to do?

Mr. Brown, knowing you to be reliable, says: "That's all right, friend Jones. You pay me the $100 cash for which I will give you a receipt, then I will take your note for six months, payable at my bank."

You agree to this; pay out the money, make and deliver the note and take the property in question, which is now yours as much as it had been his before the transfer.

The following would be a legal form in which to make the note:

$250. Summit, N. J.

October 10, 1910.

Six months after date I promise to pay to

the order of John Brown..............

Two hundred and fifty ...... dollars,....

At the Lincoln National Bank of Summit

.... Value received.

George Jones.

No. 1. Due April 14, 1911.

Now, if before the expiration of this note, you want to make a payment on it of, say, $75, you take the money to Mr. Brown, who endorses on the back of the note, "Received on the within note $75, January 3rd.," if that be the date, and signs, "John Brown."

It may be well to remember that while a running account may be collected at any time, the law cannot prevent the maker of a promissory note from selling all his belongings and leaving the country before the note is due.

DAYS OF GRACE

Notes may be "time" notes, that is where there is a specified time for payment, or "demand" notes. The latter are collectable on presentation.

With the time notes "three days grace" are allowed after the expiration of the date for payment. No such favor is allowed in the case of demand notes.

These grace days do not seem businesslike. Why not add them to the date in the note? Well, it is a custom, quite as old as the greater part of our laws, and so it must be observed.

Under the law a note is payable at the home or business place of the drawer, unless otherwise specified.

INDORSING NOTES

A note secured by a mortgage has its payment guaranteed.

The usual way of securing the payment of a note given in business is to have it endorsed with a good name across the back, as in endorsing a check.

By writing your name across the back of another man's note you announce to all the holders of that note that you know the maker and that if he does not pay it you will.

In most states the indorser of a note cannot be held responsible for payment, unless the holder notifies him, within twenty-four hours after the note comes due, that the maker cannot or will not pay.

If an indorsed note changes hands, each indorser is responsible to all endorsers who follow him and also to the last holder of the note.

If an indorser, that is, one into whose hands the note has come after the first endorsement, should not wish to guarantee payment, he writes before his name, "Without recourse to me."

This is known as a "qualified endorsement."

A NEGOTIABLE NOTE

Most notes are negotiable; that is because they may be sold, like any other personal property, or the ownership may be transferred from one person to another.

No note is negotiable that does not bear on its face, the words, "Pay to bearer," or "Pay to the order of," followed by the payee's name.

JOINT NOTES

When two persons sign a note they become jointly and individually responsible for its payment.

Such persons are known as "joint makers."

If one signs his name on the back of a note before it has been handed to the payee, he makes himself not only an endorser, but a joint maker.

If the maker of such a note refuses to pay on the expiration of time stated, he is liable for the amount without any notification.

DISCOUNTING NOTES

If a business man borrows from a bank on his note, he must pay for the privilege.

Interest is a sum paid for the use of money.

Interest is reckoned as a certain percentage yearly on the principal.

Interest on interest is called "compound interest" and is unused in ordinary business transactions.

Instead of collecting interest when the amount borrowed on a note is due, or deducting it from the principal in advance, it discounts the note at the rate agreed on and pays the rest.

This is called bank discount and its rate is variable, depending on the abundance or scarcity of money.

Money is a marketable article, and the price, like that of wheat or cotton, is governed by supply and demand.

INTEREST ON NOTES

A note may be made payable "with interest," or not, as the parties concerned may agree.

If nothing is said about interest in the note, no interest can be collected.

Again a note may go into details and specify that "the interest shall be ten per cent, payable semi-annually," provided always that the rate shall not be higher than the legal interest of the state.

Excessive interest is known as "usury." It invalidates all the interest, and in some places the principal is forfeited.

When the holder of an interest note receives interest payment he must record the date and sum on the back of the note.

PROTESTS

If a note comes due on Sunday or on a legal holiday, payment must be made on the following day.

Holidays are appointed by the separate states.

The United States recognizes no day as a holiday, except Sunday, and that is acknowledged through custom.

It is customary for banks to notify makers of notes held by them a few days before time set for payment; but this is not required by law.

If a note lies unpaid in bank the day set for payment, as soon as the office closes for regular business the note is protested.

The protest is made before a notary public; he is usually an employee of the bank.

In the protest formal objection is made against the breaking of the promise, and demanding that the matter be set right by the maker, or on his failure, by the indorser.

The indorser, who has to pay, has a claim for the amount on the maker of the note, as he would have for money loaned or goods sold, and he can sue to collect.

A note that is not paid within a fixed time is said to be "outlawed."

Remember the indorser of a note must be notified within twenty- four hours of the failure of the drawer to make good.

NOTICES

The object in protesting a note is to fix the liability on the endorser.

If there be more than one endorser notice of protest must be sent to all at the same time.

It is better, where possible, to serve the notices on the indorsers in person.

The payee must also be notified.

ACCOMMODATIONS

There is a form of note sometimes used in business which is given without any consideration on the part of the maker. This is known as an "accommodation note."

The maker of such a note does not expect to pay it, nor does the man in whose favor it is drawn expect to do so.

An accommodation note is an instrument by the sale of which, or through a bank, money may be raised for immediate use.

The maker in this case is a friend who loans his name.

As there was no value received such a note could not be collected by the payee.

But if it passes into the hands of a third party, who endorses it, then the maker of the note can be compelled to pay.

A LOST NOTE

A note may be lost or stolen.

The losing of a note does not release the maker from payment of the full amount on the date and at the place named.

The loser should at once notify the maker of his loss.

A man who buys, before its maturity, a lost or stolen note, may collect the full amount from the maker, provided the note is payable to "bearer" and no notice of the loss has been published.

When the maker of a lost note pays the amount to the original owner, he should receive from him what is known as a "bond of indemnity."

This bond is to secure him against paying a second time.

NOTES ABOUT NOTES

There are some things worth remembering about promissory notes.

1. Never give one if you can pay cash. 2. A note made on Sunday is worthless in some states. 3. A note given under compulsion is worthless. 4. Notes made by a drunken person, or obtained by any form of fraud cannot be collected under law. 5. Notes bear interest only when so stated in body of note. 6. The holder of a note has a legal claim against every indorser. 7. Each indorser is responsible to every indorser who follows him. 8. Notes are valid without reference to the kind of paper, or whether they are written with pen or pencil. 9. Losing a note does not release the maker from payment. 10.

If no time is set in a note for payment, it becomes due as soon as it is made. 11. Where a note is made in one state and is payable in another, it is governed by the laws of the state in which it is to be paid. 12. Notes payable on demand draw no interest until after they have been presented for payment. 13. If a note reads "with interest" and no rate is specified then it draws the legal interest in the state in which it was made. 14. Demand notes are not entitled to days of grace. 15. If no place of payment is named in a note, it should be presented to the maker personally in business hours. 16. The misspelling of a word or words in no way invalidates a note. 17. If a person who cannot write makes a note his mark should be properly witnessed. 18. The makers of a joint note must be sued jointly. 19. If the words and the figures in a note disagree, the words take precedence. 20. A note signed by a firm may be collected from either of the partners. 21. When a payment is made on a note secured by a mortgage, the amount is endorsed on the note, never on the mortgage. 22. A note given by a minor is void, unless given for actual necessities, like food and clothing. 23. If a note made by a minor is acknowledged when he comes of age it is binding and collectible.

CHAPTER XI

A DRAFT

A draft is a written order from the first party to the second party to pay to the third party a certain sum of money at a certain time.

The first party is called the "drawer."

The second party is the "drawee."

The third party is the "payee."

There are two kinds of draft.

The first is usually where the cashier of one bank, through his own check, draws on another bank for the cash difference in their accounts with each other.

The second form of draft is the most usual and is the one we shall here consider.

The cashier's draft is always for cash and the demand is always honored. The ordinary business draft may be for cash or for goods.

The business draft is usually honored, but there are circumstances under which it may be ignored.

TO MAKE A DRAFT

But let us suppose that the draft is all right and that a merchant, let us call him Henry Thomas, and suppose him a resident of Philadelphia, has a bill against James Taylor, of Cleveland, and he wants to collect it, without recourse to law. How will he go about it?

The bill is for $100.

Mr. Thomas writes this draft:

Philadelphia, Pa., Sept. 5, 1910.

At sight pay to the order of

Johnson National Bank of Philadelphia

One hundred................... dollars.

With exchange

and charge same to

Henry Thomas.

To James Taylor,

Cleveland, Ohio.

Having drawn his draft, Mr. Thomas takes it to the Johnson National Bank for collection. The collection is actually made by some bank in Cleveland to which the Johnson has endorsed it over.

If Mr. Thomas wished he might have sent his draft direct to the Cleveland bank, but he no doubt thought it better to transact such matters through his own bank.

Or if Mr. Thomas lived where he was not in touch with a bank, he might have drawn through any person whom he knew in Cleveland.

On receiving the draft for collection, the Cleveland bank would at once give it to a clerk who would without delay present it to Mr. Taylor.

Mr. Taylor, having written his acceptance of the draft, is given three days grace in which to make payment.

In states where days of grace are not allowed, he would have to pay at once.

Mr. Taylor writes the word "accepted," with the date and his name across the face of the draft, and if he does not pay cash, he states in the writing where payment will be made.

Of course, Mr. Taylor cannot be compelled to accept a draft. There may be good and honest reasons for his not doing so, but having accepted it, in business honor he is bound to pay it.

The term "Sight draft" explains itself, but the order to pay a draft may indicate, and often does, the number of days allowed for payment, after presentation.

FOR COLLECTION

What should be done by the man to whom a bill or a note is due, when the debtor lives in a place where there is no bank?

In that case he must learn in some way the name of a promising person to make the collection for him.

In this case he makes out the draft as before, and adds the words "for collection." This acts as a bar to any transfer of the paper.

Most banks refuse to handle a draft marked "for collection."

DISHONOR

Drafts are not necessarily duns.

Some country merchants prefer to pay their bills to wholesalers in that way, so that collecting drafts is no small part of the business of the ordinary bank.

While men are not compelled to meet drafts when presented, if the amount is due and he defaults or refuses to pay he injures his own credit.

In refusing a just draft he is said to "dishonor" it.

So sure are wholesalers that their drafts will be met by their distant debtors that they do not hesitate to draw against them when deposited for collection, regarding them as cash to their credit in bank.

PROTESTS

When a draft is not accepted or paid when due, if it be a time draft, it is protested in the same way as a note.

The protest of a draft serves as a notice to the drawer of its non-acceptance.

Like notes and checks, drafts may be transferred by a similar endorsement.

BUYING DRAFTS

If I wanted to pay a bill for $150 to Albert Holt, living at Wallace, Kansas, and did not wish to trouble him with a check, how would I go about it?

1. I might express the cash, which would be expensive. 2. I might send it in postal order, not always certain. 3. I might send it by a trusted hand, but might have long to wait before I found a friend going out to Wallace.

I am living in New York City, and am familiar enough with banking to know that New York is a great financial center and is in constant communication with nearly all the outside banks.

The outside banks keep money in deposit here, and the New York banks, particularly in the spring and autumn, keep deposits with their correspondents.

With my $150 and a small extra sum to pay my bank for drawing the draft, I go thither and buy a draft for the sum I owe Mr. Holt.

I mail this draft to my creditor and he can cash it without loss in his home bank. Here is the form:

No. 101.

Madison National Bank of New York.

Pay to the order of Albert Holt,

One hundred and fifty dollars ($150.)...

.... L. N. Jones,

Cashier.

To Prairie National Bank,

Wallace, Kansas.

A GOOD PLAN

When you buy a draft which you mean to send off in payment of a debt, a good plan is to have it made payable to yourself.

Let us suppose it is the case of Albert Holt. You transfer the draft to him by writing across the back, "Pay to the order of Albert Holt," and add your signature.

Now as all drafts are returned, as payment vouchers, to the banks from which they were issued, and as Mr. Holt must have signed the draft to get his money, it follows that there is a record of his having received it, and this has all the force of a receipt.

Do not endorse a draft with just your name, for in that case, anyone into whose hands it falls may collect. First write "Pay to the order of" the person for whom it is intended.

GOOD AS CASH

A draft made payable to yourself is as good as cash, and far safer to carry.

If you are identified at any bank between the Atlantic and

Pacific, you can have your draft cashed.

All banks furnish blank drafts.

Never endorse a draft made payable to yourself, and this applies to a check, until you are about to use it.

It is a good plan never to sign your name until it is actually necessary.

Some people have the foolish habit of signing their names on stray bits of paper.

Do not get into this habit, even if there is no space to fill out a note or order above the signature.

CHAPTER XII

JUST MONEY

As has been before stated, money in its broadest meaning is a medium of exchange.

Anything that can pay a debt or purchase property, in any part of a country, is the money of that country.

Every civilized country has its own minted or printed money.

The usual mediums of circulation are gold, silver, nickel and copper, the latter alloyed more or less in the United States with nickel.

Government and bank bills, while having all the purchasing power of gold, are simply promises to pay in gold, or other coin of "redemption", the amounts they represent.

The money of one country cannot legally be made to pay a debt in another country, unless both parties to the payment agree to it.

When gold is exchanged to settle the balances of trade between two countries, it is not reckoned, if coined, at its face value, but at its bullion value.

The word "pecunia" meant in ancient Greece and Rome a flock or herd.

In those days live stock were used as a medium of exchange, or money.

We keep the word and often use it as in "pecuniary" affairs, and when we call a moneyless man, "impecunious."

UNITED STATES MONEY

The United States Government reserves to itself the right under the constitution, to coin and issue the money to be used by its own people.

Formerly we had two standards of value, gold and silver, or bimetalism.

If gold and silver were produced in relatively equal quantities, the world would go on trading with money of both kinds, but the proportions are not the same.

Among the Aztecs and Peruvians silver ranked with gold as two to one, that is, two pounds of silver would purchase as much as one pound of gold.

But when great silver mines were discovered and new methods were discovered for extracting the metal, it became more and more abundant, till it depreciated far below the former value it had in its relation to gold.

Most of the commercial nations decided to have but one standard of value, and that gold, long before the United States fell into line.

Our money measure is known as the decimal, or metric. It would be convenient, if we could follow the example of nearly all the other commercial nations, and use the metric system for all our weights and measures.

OUR METAL MONEY

In the United States Treasury at Washington, there are many million dollars in silver coins and bullion.

The gold standard has not driven silver out of circulation, for it is still found convenient to use it in settling immediately our smaller business transactions.

When the silver dollar was first coined, and indeed up to the present date, the intention was that it should contain about a dollar's worth of silver, or 374 1/4 Troy grains of the pure metal. This amount of silver was supposed to represent permanently 24 3/4 grains of pure gold, and it did so represent its value at one time, and would have continued to do so, had the relative output of both metals been the same.

Our chief mint is in Philadelphia, where is coined all the copper, nickel, silver, and gold money in use.

To imitate these metals, even where the full value is given, constitutes the criminal offence called "counterfeiting."

In former times, some of our older readers will remember them, the Government meant to have the metal in each coin of about its unstamped value in the market.

In those days the cent was as large as our present silver half dollar, and the copper two-cent piece was a monster in the way of coinage.

Now our copper and nickel coins are small and can be carried without testing strength of pockets. They are regarded as money "tokens."

Silver coins that are punched can be refused in the settlement of a debt.

Punched gold coins should always be refused, for they are never of their face value.

Silver coins may be used in the settlement of bills up to $5.00.

Gold coins are, of course, legal tender up to any amount.

PAPER MONEY

We usually class all paper money as "bills."

There are three classes of bills, all quite different in their inception and meaning. These are—

1. National bank notes. 2. Treasury notes or "greenbacks." 3. Treasury certificates.

BANK NOTES

A national bank note is the guaranteed promise of some national bank to pay coin or its equivalent to any one presenting the note at the bank and asking to have the exchange made.

This exchange is called "redeeming."

If you examine a bank bill you will notice that it is drawn much like an ordinary business "demand" note, made payable to "bearer," and signed by the bank president and cashier.

For every dollar of its own sent out in the form of a bill by a national bank, the Government holds a dollar of the bank's collateral to guarantee the redemption of the note if the bank should fail.

National bank notes are received in all business transactions, because they are secured by the Government, yet there are cases in which even the Government will not receive them in payment of a claim, nor pay them out itself.

1. All import duties must be paid in gold. 2. The Government pays the interest on its own bonds in gold.

The Bureau of Engraving and Printing—a department of the United

States Treasury—makes and prints all the national bank notes.

On all these notes the names of the United States Treasurer and the United States Register appear. The names look like signatures, but they are facsimilies and are printed with the note.

The notes are printed on specially prepared paper, to imitate which is regarded as a counterfeit.

Soiled and worn out bank notes may be exchanged for fresh ones at the Treasury Department.

"GREENBACKS"

Greenbacks are treasury notes. The name comes from the color in which they first appeared in the years of our Civil War.

The treasury note is really an engraved promissory note of the United States Government made payable to the bearer, and bearing the signatures of the Treasurer and Register of the Treasury.

These notes are issued in denominations of from five to ten thousand dollars.

Formerly there were one and two-dollar treasury notes issued, and we still find some of these "old-timers" in circulation.

There are so many treasury notes in circulation that the Government, vast though its bullion and coin reserves are, could not redeem them if presented at once.

The treasury note is a legal tender for any amount of indebtedness.

The Government prints the following guarantee on every treasury note:

"This note is, by law, to be considered as good as coin. Any one to whom you pay it must reckon it as equivalent to a dollar (or face value in dollars) in value."

TREASURY CERTIFICATES

The treasury certificate is, in form, very much like the treasury note, and it bears the signatures of the same officers.

Treasury certificates are of two kinds, gold and silver.

The gold certificates are printed in yellow.

The silver certificates are light black and white.

These certificates are issued against the great reserves of gold and silver that are kept to redeem them.

The use of the gold certificate saves the loss of the gold that comes through abrasion when handled.

A five-dollar silver certificate is much more convenient to carry than five silver dollars.

These certificates, as may be seen, are issued for the convenience of the public.

Certificates of either character will be redeemed to any amount, in the metals for which they call, if presented at the United States Treasury at Washington, or at any of the sub-treasuries to be found in our larger cities.

WORN-OUT NOTES

Only those familiar with the work can realize the great quantities of bank bills, treasury notes, and certificates continually being made and sent out from Washington.

While a stream of clean, fresh paper of enormous value is going out to be spread all over the country, another stream of soiled, torn and altogether disreputable-looking paper is flowing back to the Treasury.

The filthy paper is quite as valuable as the clean, so it is properly checked, recorded, and credited before new paper is sent out in its place.

They are now trying to make old bills presentable by washing them at the Department. Meanwhile, most of them are ground again into pulp, made into new paper, and all the first processes gone through with to make the paper into money.

CHAPTER XIII

OUR POSTAL BUSINESS

Up to a few years ago, it was the city, town and village dweller who reaped the greatest benefit from the post office.

In dense communities carriers leave the mail at the place to which it is addressed. Where this is not done the walk for the mail is not far.

Now the purpose of our Government, which is of the people and by the people, is to treat all the people alike.

However, up to a few years ago the farmer, our most essential producer, had not a fair deal.

Fortunately things have changed and are still changing for the better.

Rural Free Delivery was an idea as just as it was grand, and as welcome as it was necessary.

The good work began October 1, 1896.

The purpose of rural free delivery is to accommodate dwellers in the country, whether farmers or not.

Through this branch of the service mails are carried daily, on fixed lines of travel, to people who otherwise would have to go long distances to reach a post office.

The Government requires that the states or counties shall keep in good condition the roads traversed by the mail carriers.

Gates must not obstruct, and it is required that every unfordable stream shall be bridged.

It is further required, as a condition for establishing a line for rural free delivery, that each route of twenty-four or more miles in length shall have at least one hundred families resident on either side.

CLASSIFIED MAIL MATTER

Mail matter is divided into four classes. For each class a different rate is charged.

First Class:—All letters, and all other written matter, with a few exceptions, pay two cents for each ounce, or fraction of an ounce.

Second Class:—Newspapers, magazines, and other periodicals, one cent for each four ounces or fraction of four ounces. Publishers of periodicals, sending direct from place of publication, get a lower rate,—one cent a pound.

Third Class:—Books, circulars, and other printed matter, one cent for two ounces or fraction of two ounces.

Fourth Class:—Merchandise and miscellaneous articles, weighing not over four pounds, one cent for each ounce or fraction of an ounce.

POSTAL RULES

1. On a tag, or the paper on which the address is written, the sender of third class matter may write "from" and add his own name and address. 2. On the blank leaf of a book, forwarded as third class matter, the sender may write a dedication or inscription, but it must not be in the form of a letter. 3. Fourth class matter must be so wrapped that the postal authorities can examine the contents without much trouble. 4. Such articles as glass, nails, needles or other matter that might work injury if it came loose, must be enclosed in two separate wrappings, or a double case. 5. Poisons, explosives, inflammable substances, and live animals are excluded from the mails. 6. Firearms may only be sent in detached parts. 7. All alcoholic liquors are regarded as explosive.

FOREIGN RATES

The rates to Canada are the same for all classes of matter as in the United States, except that seeds, scions, bulbs, cuttings, and roots are one cent per ounce.

To Cuba all the rates are the same as for domestic matter.

Rates with Mexico are the same as if mailed between our own states. Packages are limited to 4 pounds 6 ounces, except that single books may weigh more. Merchandise must be sent by parcel post.

To all other countries, in what is known as the "Postal Union", the rates for letters are five cents for each half ounce or fraction thereof.

Postal cards two cents each, double four cents.

Registration fees or letters or other articles, four cents each.

Ordinary letters for foreign countries, except Canada, Cuba and Mexico, must be forwarded, whether any postage is paid on them or not.

All other mailable matter must be prepaid.

Alaska, Hawaii, Guam, Tetuila, the Philippines and Porto Rico are regarded as insular or territorial possessions of the United States, and are entitled to the same postal rates.

STAMPS

Postage stamps may be purchased at any United States post office, or at any place authorized to sell them.

Anyone may sell postage stamps as he would any other personal asset.

If stamps are bought to be enclosed in a letter, they should never be of a higher denomination than twos and ones, as they are easily disposed of.

Letters should always be stamped on the upper right-hand corner of the envelope.

Packages should be stamped in the same way and on the addressed side.

The using of cancelled stamps is a felony.

Foreign stamps have no value on letters or parcels mailed in the

United States.

A domestic, unstamped letter will not be forwarded.

If a stamped letter is found to require more postage, the amount lacking is stamped on the letter, and must be paid by the receiver.

Stamped envelopes and stamped wrappers are sold by the post office at the usual rates of postage, with the cost of the paper added.

If a stamped envelope or wrapper is spoiled, the stamp must not be cut off and used by pasting on another envelope or wrapper, for it will be treated as if no postage were paid.

Such spoiled wrappers or envelopes will be exchanged, without charge, by the postmaster, for stamps of the same value.

POSTAL CARDS

Never use a postal card to dun a debtor.

Never send a confidential message on a postal card.

Foreign postal cards, that is those bearing a foreign stamp, cannot be used in the United States.

An international postal card can be bought.

Postal cards and letters may be redirected and forwarded without extra charge, where the address of the receiver has been changed. Packages require a renewal of payment in such cases.

REGISTERING LETTERS

A letter or a parcel may be registered to further insure its safe delivery.

When a letter or parcel is registered, it must have the sender's name and address written across the left-hand end of the envelope and on the reverse side.

In addition to the stamps required ordinarily, eight cents in stamps or in a regularly prepared stamp, is the registration fee.

The clerk, receiving a registered parcel, gives the sender a receipt for the same. After the letter has reached its destination, the sender gets a second receipt, through the post office, signed with the receiver's name.

The receiver of a registered parcel signs two receipts, one for the post office and the other for the sender.

SPECIAL DELIVERY

The purpose of what is known, in connection with the post office, as the "Special Delivery System", is to insure the delivery of any letter or package to the person, to whom it is addressed, as soon as it reaches his post office.

In addition to the regular post charge, a fee of 10 cents is added for special delivery. This is in the form of a special stamp, though when this cannot be had, the same amount in ordinary stamps may be attached.

In the case noted, the sender should write in line with the stamps, "special delivery."

Special delivery messages are delivered, not by ordinary carriers, but by special delivery messengers.

The special delivery letter is used when immediate knowledge is necessary. It saves a long telegram.

MONEY ORDERS

Money, in limited sums, may be sent through the post office. One advantage of sending money in this way is that it practically insures the sender against loss.

All post offices are not money order offices.

A post office money order may only be sent to those places where there are such offices.

At all post offices, authorized to send money orders, proper blanks can be had on which the sender can write his order.

Any sum may be sent by postal order, from one cent to one hundred dollars.

The fee is from three to thirty cents.

Read the blank carefully; it is simple, but be sure you understand it before filling out the order.

If in doubt, ask the clerk.

Having filled out the order, hand it to the clerk with the sum required, and the additional fee.

The clerk then prepares and hands out an order for the amount, on the postmaster of the town to which you are sending your letter, and this you enclose to your correspondent.

CASHING POST OFFICE ORDERS

The money order never contains the name of the sender; this the postmaster of the office from which it is sent supplies in a separate communication to the postmaster who is to pay.

No money passes from one office to the other.

A post office order is like a draft drawn by one postmaster on another. The one credits the sum, the other debits it.

The holder of an order will not get his money unless he is known to the paying postmaster or is identified.

Before paying an order the postmaster requires the holder to receipt it.

A post office money order, like a check or draft, may be transferred to another for collection.

Banks receive transferred money orders as if they were cash deposits.

The party to whom orders are transferred must go through the same forms at the office, where payment is made, as if he was the original payee.

ADVICE

It is not necessary to register letters containing checks. Never write "personal" on a business letter.

Always enclose a stamp for reply when writing to a stranger.

See that the addresses on your letters are distinctly legible.

CHAPTER XIV

TELEGRAMS—THE TELEPHONE

To send a telegram, you or your messenger must take what you have written to the nearest telegraph office.

You may write a telegram on any kind of paper, provided always that the writing is plain.

All telegraph offices are provided with regular blank forms, which may be had without cost, and it is better to use these when they are available.

The blank is properly ruled, with lines for the date, for the address of the one to whom it is to be sent, and for the message.

CHARGES

The telegraph company charges a fixed sum for a message of, say, ten words. These words do not include the name and address of the sender.

The amount of the charge is always dependent on the distance between the office from which the message is sent and the one at which it is received.

Every word over ten, in the message, pays an extra fee, dependent again on the distance.

Getting just what you mean into ten words may seem difficult when you have a lot to say, but it is surprising how you can boil the message down when each additional word costs five or more cents.

It may pay to practice this.

If it is actually necessary to make your meaning clear by the addition of more words, do not hesitate at the cost.

If you are known at the telegraph office, you can send a message to be collected from the receiver.

Never permit the receiver to pay for a message that is exclusively on your own business.

Always make and keep a copy of every important telegram you send away. Do not neglect this.

If you have neglected to keep a copy of a telegram, or having made one have lost it, you may get a copy from the telegraph office, provided the application be made within six months of the sending of the message.

Telegrams are delivered by the company's messengers.

You must give receipt to the messenger on the delivery of a telegram.

Where the receiver lives a long distance from the telegraph office, it is customary to pay the messenger an additional fee, depending on the distance.

The charges for telegrams to be sent at night and delivered in the morning, are much lower than for day messages.

For an additional charge, less than the original, messages may be repeated back to insure their accuracy.

Read over to the official, or still better, have him read your message over in your presence, that you may be sure he understands it as written.

You cannot hold others responsible for your own mistakes.

TELEGRAPHING MONEY

You can telegraph money with as much safety as you can send it through a bank.

In handling money in this way, the telegraph company does not act as a banker but as a carrier.

Telegraph money orders are a great convenience, when one wants to send cash to a distant point in a hurry.

Country telegraph offices do not, as a rule, transmit money; that function is left to the offices in the larger centers.

THE METHOD

One wishing to "wire money" will find at the telegraph office suitable blanks; they are furnished gratis.

On lines provided for the purpose and properly indicated, as in a postal order form, write the name and address of the person to receive the money, with the amount.

This paper, properly signed, is handed to the clerk with the money to be sent and the fee for transmission.

The fee is double that charged for an ordinary message of the same length.

If, for any reason, the person to whom the money is sent cannot be found within forty-eight hours, the money is returned to the sender, but the fees are retained, as the company is not to blame for failure.

The receiver of a money order, if unknown, must identify himself as he would at a bank, and he must receipt for the money.

If the person to receive the money is an entire stranger in the place to which the money is sent, the sender knows it, and he provides for the situation by signing, on the reverse of the application, an order to the distant operator to pay the money to the person named within, without further identification.

When a telegraph operator receives a money order, he at once seeks out the person to whom it is sent, and pays the money in accordance with his instructions as to identification.

THE TELEPHONE

The telephone, local and long distance, is fast superceding the telegraph as a medium for speedy business communications.

Its use is not confined to large cities as at first.

Nearly every village is now in communication with the outer world through the telephone.

The world has just awakened to the needs of its food producer, the farmer.

In Norway, which is not a rich country, the telephone has been introduced on the farms. The rates are low and the benefits are inestimable.

On our large farms, in the West, telephones have been in use for some time as an essential part of the machinery.

Now, there is a move on foot to make them available for every farmer in the more settled regions.

While business can be conducted over the telephone, as if the speakers stood face to face, yet such transactions not being recorded, will not stand in law, if one of the parties should dispute the other's word.

CHAPTER XV

BUSINESS BY EXPRESS

There are two kinds of expresses, viz.: local and general. The names describe the provinces of each, though a general express may do a local business.

All express companies are common carriers.

The carrying business done by our express companies is enormous. They have their own special cars attached to passenger and fast freight trains, and their goods are given special departments in water transportation.

If living between two towns, it is always better to have your letters and express business done through one office.

INSTRUCTIONS

When ordering material by express, make sure that you give the address, to which you wish it sent, in such a way that a mistake on the part of the forwarder will be out of the question.

If you send away goods by express, make sure that they are securely packed, and be equally sure that the address is clearly written and in a large hand. It would be better if the address could be painted on with a brush.

If you should send perishable stuff, like meat, flowers, glass, or fruit, be sure to label the package "perishable" or "Handle with care, glass."

On long distance transportation prepayment is required; on short distances it is optional.

It is always better to get from the express agent a receipt for the matter taken in charge.

Take care to put your own address on the lower left-hand corner of the package to be sent.

If the person to whom the parcel is sent cannot be found, the address will enable the express company to notify the sender at once of the fact.

When sending any goods by express, it is always prudent to notify the person for whom they are intended of the fact by mail, and also to state the company by which the matter was sent and the date of shipment.

THE COMPANY'S DUTY

The express company must always require, on delivering goods, a receipt from the receiver.

If the goods should be received by a second person, on behalf of the consignee, he must sign the consignee's name, and under that his own.

If a package appears to be damaged in transmission, the express company must permit the receiver to examine it before signing. He may refuse to sign or to accept in any way, if the goods are injured, or not as he ordered.

Express companies are responsible for all damages sustained by goods while in their charge.

COLLECTIONS BY EXPRESS

All the large express companies have the machinery for collecting accounts and notes whenever they have branch offices.

Such companies are reliable collectors. Their services are prompt and their charges reasonable.

Where an express company fails to collect, notice is promptly given with the reasons for failure.

When you wish an express company to collect, it will be necessary for you to make out a statement of the account. This is placed in a special envelope, provided by the company. It is properly indorsed and handed to the company's representative.

The company charges a small fee for collection, whether it succeeds or not. In any case the fee is not much above a fourth of one per cent, unless there should be unusual trouble.

C. O. D. BY EXPRESS

As you know, C.O.D. means "cash on delivery".

Cash on delivery orders constitute no small part of every express company's business.

When goods are forwarded in this way, the sender furnishes with the goods an itemized bill duly receipted. The express company's charges should be included in the bill.

The express agent is sure to collect the bill before he lets the goods leave his keeping.

MONEY BY EXPRESS

Should you desire to send money by express, it will be well to go to the company's office before you pack it up.

Express companies have special receptacles or envelopes in which to store coin or bills. There is no charge for these.

The sender must himself seal the packages containing the money, and write on them the address of the consignee, also the amount enclosed.

Having received the packages, the express agent ties them up, affixes his official seal, which is so arranged that the package cannot be opened or tampered with, without breaking. This done, he gives the sender a receipt. This should be cared for as a vital part of the record.

The charges for sending money by express may or may not be paid in advance. They vary with the amount to be carried and the distance.

Packages of money are receipted for in the usual way. They are delivered only to the legal consignee, unless a second person should appear with an order, amounting to a power of attorney, and which the company cannot reject.

MONEY ORDERS

The foregoing by no means limits the express company's usefulness or field of opportunities.

Express companies issue money orders much as does the Post Office

Department.

As with the post office, the fees for orders vary, but no order is issued for more than fifty dollars.

If you want to send such an order, the express company will furnish the proper blank for you to fill out.

On this form must be written out very plainly the name and address of the person to whom the order is to be sent, with the amount, in words and in figures.

On receiving the money the express agent gives to his customer two papers; one is the company's receipt for the money, the other is the order itself.

The order instructs the agent at the point to which it is to be sent to pay the sum named to the person named.

To complete the order the sender should sign his name in a place indicated for the purpose on the back of the paper.

This done, the order can be sent to the person for whom it is intended, in an ordinary envelope.

The receiver of an express money order can have it cashed at the express office in his town, or sign it and place it in his own bank as if it were cash.

CHAPTER XVI

ABOUT RAILROADS

Not everything about railroads, that would be a tremendous undertaking, but just enough to show what everyone should know about them as carriers of goods.

The express companies have practically a monopoly of the transportation of the smaller packages of goods requiring quick transit and immediate delivery, but the longer, heavier, and slower freight are in the hands of the railroads, and where it can be done, and time is not a first factor, the steamboat takes the place of the train.

BILLS OF LADING

As most of the goods in changing hands are carried by steamboat or railroad, the method of shipment should be understood by everyone who may be called on to use one or the other means of transportation.

The person shipping goods in this way is the "consignor."

The person to whom the goods are shipped is the "consignee".

The goods shipped are described in a paper called a "bill of lading."

A bill of lading is a written contract, or statement of the goods shipped, their condition, and the time of shipment.

Bills of lading and receipt blanks are furnished at the offices of the transportation companies.

Two copies of the bill of lading should be made out. One of these is signed by the consignor and the other by the transportation agent.

The copy signed by the consignor is kept by the agent, and the copy signed by the agent is retained by the consignor, as a voucher for the goods shipped.

This receipt should be mailed to the consignee.

When the consignee gets this bill of lading, it is a voucher to the freight agent, where the goods are to be delivered, as to the ownership.

It is usual for the agent at the point of shipment to send a copy of the bill of lading to the agent where the goods are received. In this way he can compare the consignment with the consignee's bill.

EXPENSE BILLS

It is not usual to pay freight bills at the point of shipment, that being left till the goods reach their destination.

The agent at the place of delivery makes out an "expense bill," which is an itemized statement of the freight charges, and must be paid by the consignee before delivery.

This done, the consignee must sign a receipt for the goods delivered, and the affair is closed.

A BILL AND A DRAFT

Before wholesale houses or manufacturers ship goods, they are either paid for or they have a business understanding with the consignee as to when and how the payment is to be made.

There are occasions, however, when no such arrangement has been made, and a man not well known to the merchant orders goods shipped by freight.

In a case like this, the merchant may ascertain through a commercial agency—the agencies make it their business to keep posted in such matters—the standing of the man giving the order.

Trade has its risks and the merchant, even where the information is not quite assuring, may decide to fill the order and ship it.

As with express companies, goods may be sent as freight, C. O. D.

This is done by means of a bill of lading, to which is attached a draft. The shipper bills the goods to himself at the point to which they were ordered.

To the bill of lading he attaches a draft for the sum involved, but this, instead of being forwarded to the consignee by mail, is sent to him through a bank for collection.

Now before the consignee can get the bill of lading, which authorizes him to receive the goods, he must pay the draft.

The bill, which is in the shipper's name, is then endorsed over to the payer of the draft.

Country merchants and sometimes farmers send produce by freight to be sold on commission in the city.

AN INVOICE

Delhi, N. Y., Sept. 9, 1910.

Invoice of Merchandise shipped by

Harry T. Jackson

and consigned to Brown, Smith & Co.,

Newburg, N. Y.

to be sold on commission.

120 bbls. Potatoes

70 " green apples

40 Crates tomatoes.

Mark plainly all goods shipped.

CHAPTER XVII

TAXES

Generally speaking, tax bills are paid with reluctance.

This is no doubt due to the fact that with every other form of payment one has something tangible to show for the expenditure.

If every good citizen could be brought to see that his private interests are closely linked with public affairs, he would take more interest in the local politics of his town and county, and so have a voice in the expenditure of taxes by selecting the best men to do the work for him.

Taxes are forced contributions levied on citizens to provide money for public expenses, such as law and order, schools, charities and public institutions.

All tax laws are made by the men who pay the taxes.

You say "No" to this.

"The tax laws are made by the legislators up at the state capital."

Very true; but who nominates and elects the legislators? Did you not put them into office?

"No, the bosses did that," you reply.

True again, but good men are in the majority and if they did their duty to their country and themselves, there would be no bosses and taxes would be honestly spent.

KINDS OF TAXES

Tax laws are enacted by Congress, and by the legislatures of our many states. Taxes cannot be collected without this authority.

State taxes are collected for the state use only.

United States taxes are expended for the benefit of all the people of all the states.

Taxes may be further divided into direct and indirect.

Direct taxes are, at present, only employed by the states. They are levied on realty and personal property, and are paid by the particular person named in the tax bill presented by the authorized collector.

The amount of these taxes vary each year, depending on the public requirements.

They are based on assessments made by officers appointed for the purpose and generally known as assessors.

CUSTOMS DUTY

Though there is no demand made on each individual to pay the indirect taxes required by the Government, yet indirectly every person who spends little or much money is paying them.

The Government's chief means of raising the great sums of money needed yearly to carry on its machinery is by customs duties and internal revenue collections.

The customs revenue is obtained from a tax levied on certain articles imported from foreign countries.

This customs tax is called a tariff.

The question as to the goods that shall be subject to a tariff and the amount to be levied on the same, is one that has long perplexed statesmen and been a leading party issue.

The merchant, to whom the goods are assigned from a foreign port, must pay the duty levied on them by a Government Appraiser before he can take them away.

Private parties, landing from abroad at any of our ports of entry, are required, before getting their baggage, to write out a declaration of the things contained in their trunks. But this declaration does not prevent the customs inspectors from making a careful personal examination. All things found dutiable, whether declared or not, are set apart and held until the assessment or duty is paid.

The evasion of a customs duty is called "smuggling" and is punished by the confiscation of the goods, and penalties in the way of fine and imprisonment.

There are people who would consider it a sin to cheat their butcher, but see no wrong in cheating the Government.

To the merchant who pays tariff duties the amount involved is a direct tax.

When the merchant sells his goods to the retailer or consumer, he adds the tariff to his freight, insurance, interest, etc., as direct purchase cost. This is strict business, but the consumer pays all the bills with the profit added.

INTERNAL REVENUE

The second great source of Government revenue is derived from the internal revenue tax, or excise duties.

Manufacturers of alcohol, whether as wine, whiskey, or beer, and the producers of tobacco, in its manufactured forms, have to pay an excise tax in proportion to the amount and character of their products.

As with the customs tax, the excise tax is added by the manufacturer to the cost of production, so that at last it is the consumer who pays it.

STAMPS

While the manufacturers of alcohol pay the excise tax in bulk, that is on the number of gallons produced, the manufacturers of cigars and tobacco have to attach to each separate package a distinct internal revenue stamp.

These stamps are purchased from the internal revenue collectors, appointed by the Government to certain districts. The stamps show at a glance that the proper tax has been paid, just as the postage stamp affixed to a letter proves that the price for carrying it and delivering it has been paid.

As it is a penal offence to use a postage stamp a second time, so it is a punishable offence to attempt the use of a cancelled or torn internal revenue stamp.

If demanded, the Government will give a receipt for the sum received from any one for considerable sales of postal or revenue stamps.

STATE TAXES

State taxes, as has been stated, are levied on real and personal property. Some states have in addition a poll tax. This is levied on the individual without any regard to his property, and a receipt for it may be a requirement before a citizen is permitted to vote.

Of course the real estate and personal property taxes are not the same in all the states, for each state must raise every year the sum necessary to meet its own special requirements.

The intention of all tax laws is to have every citizen's contribution bear the same proportion to the whole amount to be raised that his possessions bear to the aggregate property of all the owners in the commonwealth.

EXEMPT FROM TAXES

All our state laws exempt from taxation certain kinds of property.

The state cannot tax the property held by itself for the common use.

The buildings and related properties of religious bodies and societies are not taxable.

Such educational institutions as colleges, seminaries, and private charities are not taxed.

Cemeteries and other places where the dead are disposed of are not taxed.

County buildings, city parks, public schools, penal institutions, fair grounds for public use and similar property is never taxed.

INSUFFICIENT TAXES

There have been times in the life of the Government, and in the building up of the states, when the funds necessary for maintenance from taxes, heavy though these have been at times, have not been sufficient to meet the essential expenditures.

This was particularly the case with our Government during the trying days of our Civil War.

States entering on great public works, for the benefit of the commonwealth, frequently cannot raise the necessary money by the usual forms of taxation.

In these cases loans have to be made, that is the Government and the state go out and borrow from those who have it to spare, the necessary money.

The Government, the state, and it may be the city or county, gives to the party providing the money what is known as bond or bonds, each of a fixed amount and bearing a fixed rate of interest, payable as a rule semi-annually.

PERSONAL PROPERTY

There is no form of property so easy to assess for the purpose of taxation as real estate, that is the land and the buildings, for the last selling value of this property is a matter of public record, and then the assessors, who should be men of honesty and good judgment, are generally posted as to the value of the property under consideration.

When, however, it comes to the taxation of personal property, which means any kind of property that can be detached and carried about, it is a different matter.

Just as many people, otherwise regarded as honest, do not think it a great wrong to get the better of the Custom House, so many reputable people are inclined to revolt against the tax on personal property and to conceal their actual possessions from the assessor, nor is this peculiarity confined to the poor.

Any man may be legally compelled to swear to the accuracy of his statement, and if it is found that he has knowingly sworn to a false statement, he may be brought to task for perjury.

What is known as "personal property" varies in many of the states.

Personal property generally includes, merchandise in possession; all fixtures, all furniture in home, offices, and factories; all live stock, all money on hand and in banks; other men's notes, not transferred; all stocks and bonds and other forms of security.

TOWN TAXES

Townships or counties, if properly authorized by charter or the votes of the people, may levy special taxes for special purposes within the limits of their own jurisdictions, or they may in the same way sell bonds to carry out some work that has been decided on for the common weal.

Two or more towns, or counties, may join in the same way to carry out a project of benefit to both, provided that the burden of the undertaking be equitably assessed.

PAYMENTS

All tax bills are due and collectable on presentation, but this is never enforced.

A time is, however, fixed beyond which payment cannot be deferred.

A sufficient amount of any property may be sold at auction to satisfy a tax bill.

Of old, and still in some places, the road taxes were paid in cash, but more frequently by work on the roads, either by the individual man, or in connection with his team, each day's work of one or both being fixed at a regular rate.

TAXING CORPORATIONS

The state does not tax the individual members of a corporation for property held in common. The same result is secured better by taxing the corporation as a body. This applies to banks, railroads, and incorporated manufacturing establishments.

Savings banks are taxed lightly. Every depositor is liable for a personal property tax proportioned to the amount of his credit.

To make collection easy the savings bank always pays the amount of this tax in bulk, and then charges it to the expense account of the establishment, so that indirectly the depositors pay after all, as their dividends are reduced by just the amount of the tax.

TAXES IN GENERAL

When a man owns property in different towns, counties, or states, he is regarded as so many individuals, and must pay each as the local demands require. No matter where a man's personal property is placed, the rule is to tax him for the whole at the place of his usual residence.

The landlord and the merchant each pays a direct tax to the collector, but it would be a business error to think that in so doing either or both is carrying more than his share of the total taxation.

The landlord keeps in mind the added expense when he comes to adjust leases with his tenants. The merchant, who pays taxes on his stock and so adds to his expense account, should not be blamed if he keeps this in mind when he fixes the selling prices of his goods.

THE RETURNS

Taxes duly paid, honestly collected, and properly expended should never be regarded as a burden.

From no equal expenditure of money do the people get so much good.

The public schools, the public highways, the protection of life and property, public hospitals, public libraries, residences for the old, the blind, the orphaned and the insane, as well as secure places for the lawless, are built and maintained by the taxpayer.

As a rule all these things are done honestly and well, notwithstanding the outcry to the contrary.

If there be dishonesty in places, it is the fault quite as much of the voter who selected him as of the official culprit himself.

We must take all the responsibility of our agents, whether they be public or private.

Every good citizen should feel that his public duty is an important private business.

CHAPTER XVIII

CONTRACTS, LEASES, AND GUARANTEES

The law books define a contract to be "An agreement between two or more persons to do or not to do a certain stated thing or things, for a consideration."

The consideration is a vital part of every contract.

There can be no binding contract without a consideration.

The other requisites of a contract are—

1. It must be possible of accomplishment. 2. It must be in accordance with law. 3. Its performance must not injure the public. 4. The parties to a contract must be competent to do the things to which they pledge themselves. 5. A drunken or an insane man cannot make a contract. 6. All parties to a contract must be agreed.

THE CONSIDERATION

No contract can be held as binding where the consideration is not named.

A promise, verbal or in writing, to do something for a certain party, cannot be enforced.

A promise to do the same thing for a stipulation named is a contract and may be enforced.

A gift is not a form of contract. Once made it cannot be legally taken back.

WRITTEN AND VERBAL CONTRACTS

There are certain forms of contract which cannot be legally enforced, unless they are in writing.

1. All contracts for the sale of real estate. 2. Contracts that are not to be performed for a year or more. 3. All contracts, to answer for the debt and obligations of another, must be in writing.

If the contracting parties put but a part of their agreement in writing the law will recognize only the written part. The whole must be in writing, or the agreement will not hold.

Verbal contracts are not safe.

Although the law does not require even contract to be in writing, yet, as it never declares that a contract must be verbal, it is the part of prudence, wherever possible, to put every contract in writing.

Owing to defects of memory even honest men may, and frequently do, disagree as to the terms of a verbal contract.

Because the party with whom the contract is made is a close friend, one is apt to depend on a verbal agreement, but the closer the friend or relative, the more reason there is for an exact written contract, if we would keep the friend.

FORMS OF CONTRACT

The law is never specific as to the form of contract that may be used.

It is not necessary to draw up the contract with the formal accuracy of a real estate deed.

Any one with good sense and a fair common school education can draw up a contract that will hold.

Know what is required, then state the facts simply.

Contracts need not be sworn to or even witnessed.

KINDS OF CONTRACT

Every note, mortgage and other form of obligation is a specific contract.

A lease is a form of contract between two people, known as landlord and tenant, for the use of real estate for a period and at a rental specified in the document.

A verbal lease may be made for a short period, but if for a year or more, it must be in writing.

A lease should state when, where and to whom the rent is to be paid.

Each party to a lease, or other form contract should have a copy.

If the premises rented should become unusable by fire or any action of the elements the tenant is still liable for rent, unless there is a special clause in the lease providing for such a contingency.

A tenant cannot, without the written consent of the landlord, use the rented premises for any other purpose than that stated in the lease.

AS TO REPAIRS

In some states the law compels the landlord to keep the premises in habitable repair, but this does not seem to be the rule. It should be decided, where there is doubt, before signing the lease.

Where it is agreed that the landlord shall keep the premises in repair, and, after due notice of the fact, he fails to do so, the tenant may himself make the repairs and deduct the amount from the rent.

SUBLETTING

If there is no contract to the contrary, the tenant may sublet the whole or any part of the premises, but this does not release him from liability for rent.

If the tenant fails to leave the property when his lease has expired, the owner may make his demand through what is known as a "notice to quit," which must be served on the tenant in person.

WHAT IS A GUARANTY?

A guaranty is sometimes required to insure the payment of rent.

Plainly, a guaranty is an agreement to assume, under certain conditions, the liabilities of another.

If a man makes a contract, a lease, or a note, and his personal resources are not deemed sufficient to secure his performance of the things agreed to, the other may require that some one, in whom he has more faith, shall give him a guaranty, or personal security in writing.

The following might be used as the form for a guaranty for a lease, contract, note or other obligation of contract:

"For value received, I hereby guarantee

the payment of the within lease (bond or

contract). George L. Roberts."

Short Hills, N. J.

October 1, 1910.

A BILL OF SALE

This is a written agreement by which one person transfers to another his interest in certain personal property.

The law lays down no rule as to the form.

A bill of sale usually passes where the property paid for is not immediately removed from the possession of the seller.

This form would answer in any state:

"Bridgeport, Conn., Aug. 2, 1910.

"I have this day sold to Calvin E. Platt,

of New Haven, in this state, my team of

bay horses, with their harness, one family

carriage, and a two-seated cutter.

"Thomas P. Fletcher."

Be sure, where the bill of sale includes many articles, to name every one of them in the bill.

If paid for, whether by cash or a note, be sure to get a receipt for the same.

OBLIGATIONS

A bond is a form of obligation.

Every enforcible bond must be in writing and under seal.

The maker of a bond by the act acknowledges a liability in the form of a debt or a duty.

The maker of a bond is the "obligor."

The party to whom it is made is the "obligee."

The bond names the liability or indebtedness; then follows the condition wherein it is stated the particular thing that the obligor is to do, or not to do.

The penalty for the non-compliance with a bond is twice the amount of the money involved.

It is often required that the bond shall be further guaranteed by one or more sureties. These sureties may be required to certify that they are worth a certain sum, free and clear of all indebtedness.

Persons holding positions of financial trust, whether public or private, may be, and most of them are, required to furnish bonds for the faithful performance of their duties.

In the larger cities there are casualty and liability companies, which, for a fixed or annual consideration, act as sponsors on official and other forms of bond.

Where there are no such companies, as those just named, then private citizens of known responsibility must be secured to go on the bond.

In every case the amount of the bond or security is measured by the responsibilities of the man from whom it is required.

CHAPTER XIX

LIFE INSURANCE

Life insurance may be defined to be "A contract for the future payment of a certain sum of money to a person specified in the body of the policy, on conditions dependent on the length of some particular person's life."

There are two parties to this contract—the insured and the insurer.

The purpose of the insurer, if he take out the policy in his own name, is to provide in a measure for the care of his family, or other dependents, in the event of his death.

After a long experience with the death rates in all lands that keep mortuary statistics, the actuaries of insurance companies can now estimate with surprising accuracy the probable length of life before any man of any age.

The methods of insurance companies mean to be scientific, but be that as it may, they are certainly interesting.

HOW IT IS DONE

Let us take a young man of thirty, married, with one child, in good health, and in receipt of a fair salary, but with no property to leave his wife and little one in the event of his death.

To secure his dear ones, he decides to insure his life for, let us say, $3,000.

He fills out the blank, in which his age and all the other required information is given; then the insurance company's doctor examines him and he is accepted as what is called "a good risk."

Now, from its actuary tables, the company knows, with reasonable accuracy, the number of years this young man should live, barring accidents.

Already they have their tables of calculations for such cases. They know what expense will be required in the way of rent, clerks, advertising, etc., to care for this case till the prospective, the inevitable end is reached.

On these calculations the immediate and all subsequent premiums or payments are based.

The insurance company invests and reinvests the premiums, and the total of these, it is estimated, will meet the expenses and the amount of the policy at the time of its calculated expiration.

AS AN INVESTMENT

If the young man in question had the money, he would find it to his advantage to buy a paid up policy, that is one on which no further premiums would be required.

But, having the money for a paid up policy, could not the young man, without any expense for clerk hire or rent, invest it, and reinvest it with the interest, as long as he lived, and thus make by insuring himself?

There can be no question as to that, provided always that the young man lived out the calculated time, invested his insurance money at once, and kept on investing it in "safe things" as long as he lived. But how many young men are there who could or would take this course?

It is much easier to save from our earnings than it is to invest those earnings wisely.

FORMS OF LIFE INSURANCE

The straight life policy, payable to the heirs at death, is the form in general use, but there are others.

There is yet another form, known as the "endowment," which in itself combines the usual life insurance with some of the privileges of a savings bank.

The endowment policy, while payable if death should occur before a fixed time, specifies the date when it shall be payable to the insured himself, if he should live till that time.

In this case the family is secured, in the event of death, and the insured has a guarantee for himself when he reaches life's unproductive years.

The premiums on an endowment policy are necessarily greater than those on a regular life, and the premiums increase with the shortness of the time.

MUTUAL INSURANCE SOCIETIES

Seeing the vast sums accumulated by what are known as "the old line companies," despite their high salaries and great expenses, working men throughout the world, but more particularly in the United States, have banded together and formed mutual insurance companies.

These companies, there are many of them, are known as societies, and their local branches are called "lodges," "councils" or a similar name.

Properly conducted, these mutual societies should be able to furnish insurance at about actual cost, for the expenses of management and collections are small.

It can be said that some of them have been and are being well managed, but others, like their predecessors, the old line companies, have unfortunately been conducted for the enrichment of their promoters.

The mutual insurance companies, like their more pretentious prototypes, are now placed under the supervision of inspectors in nearly all the states.

AMOUNTS OF POLICIES

In the society companies, there is a limit to the amount, usually $3,000, for which one can be insured, but the regular companies have no such limitation.

In the mutual insurance companies, the insured cannot leave his insurance to his creditors, or to any one not within a certain degree of kinship.

In the regular companies a man may insure for any amount he thinks he can carry, and he can insure in the same way in any number of companies, and he can leave the money to any one he may select, or for any purpose he may choose.

Sometimes the policy is made payable to unnamed executors. These may be named in a will made after he has taken out his policy.

POLICIES AS SECURITY

Sometimes a man, without real estate or other personal assets, desires to raise a loan on his life insurance, which, it should be said, is a form of personal property. In this case he may assign his life policy, or his endowment policy, as security for the loan.

Again, if he is not insured and has no shadow of an asset, he may have his life insured for the benefit of another, in consideration for a loan.

LAPSES

When there is a failure to meet premiums, the policy is said to "lapse" or default.

Even in this case the insured has an equity.

Every policy, depending on the amount paid, has what is known as a "surrender value," and by proper process this may be collected from the company.

In some states, if the insured fails to meet his premiums, the company is compelled to pay on the policy at his death a sum equivalent to that which he paid before default.

Some insurance policies have a clause stating that the contract will be void in the event of the suicide of the holder. The highest courts have set this clause aside. The ruling is that a suicide is an insane man, and that his heirs should not be made to suffer for his misfortune.

PROPRIETARY AND MUTUAL COMPANIES

The larger insurance companies may be either proprietary or mutual, some are a combination of both.

The proprietary companies are corporations organized by a number of men to conduct life insurance as a business enterprise.

Such a company must be regularly chartered, and is under the supervision of the state department of insurance.

Mutual companies, as the name implies, are organized and are meant to be managed for the benefit of the policy holders, who are also regarded as stock holders, with the right to vote in the election of officers and other company affairs.

Aiming to create a strong reserve fund to secure the policy holders, the mutual life insurance companies usually charge a little more in the way of premiums.

Many rich men have their lives insured for great amounts. This is done that their heirs may not be forced to break up the estate, at death, in order to settle the ordinary liabilities.

If it can be afforded, it is always well to carry some life insurance.

CHAPTER XX

FIRE AND ACCIDENT INSURANCE

We hear and know much about life insurance because, no doubt, it has to do directly with the individual, and so has a personal appeal; but there are other forms of insurance, forms that have to do with things material, that play an important part in the world's business.

LIKE GAMBLING

The gambling spirit, like the desire for stimulants and the tobacco habit, seems to be well nigh universal.

Men bet on the turn of dice, the cutting of cards, or the tossing of a coin, and we very properly denounce it as gambling. We take money without giving an equivalent, or we part with it and have nothing to show for the transfer.

There are insurance companies in England and in other parts of Europe where they insure risks from life to fire, from ships to crops, and from the turning of a card to the tossing of a coin.

The English company, known the world over as "Lloyd's," is ready to insure an ocean liner, or to guarantee that the next child born into your family will be a boy or a girl; it will even insure that there will or will not be twins, and that, if twins, they will be boys or girls, or one of each.

Now, this looks like gambling, and you would be quite right in so classing it, yet it is founded on the well considered law of chance, and the premiums—call them bets—are calculated with a mathematical precision surprising to one who has not studied the matter.

WHAT IS FIRE INSURANCE?

Fire insurance is a contract between the insured and the company taking the risk, in which for a consideration called a "premium," the company agrees to pay to the insured a stated sum, should the property, named in the policy, be destroyed by fire.

If there should be a fire, during the life of the policy, and the damage is not total, the company pays only enough to cover the loss.

Should the property be totally destroyed the company pays up to the amount named in the policy.

No company cares to insure for the full amount of the property; that might be an incentive to incendiarism.

In taking a fire risk, the companies base their estimates on tables as carefully worked out and from experiences quite as well studied as those of the actuaries of life companies.

Fire companies are purely business corporations, and their conduct is subject to the inspection of the officials of the state from which they receive their charters.

PREMIUMS

As life companies have rates dependent on the age of the insured, so fire companies regulate their premiums by the location and other circumstances of the buildings; in other words, they calculate the probabilities, and charge accordingly.

There are buildings particularly subject to combustion on which American companies will not take a risk. Among these may be classed kerosene and turpentine stills, sulphur and powder mills, and the buildings in which these products are stored.

Buildings not used for the purposes named, but in close proximity to them, are often considered too dangerous to warrant the issuance of a policy.

In all cases, the company makes a careful survey of the property to be insured, and on this report the amount of the premium is based.

Premiums on fire policies must be paid in bulk and in advance.

Policies should be renewed some days before the expiration of the old ones.

Fire premiums, taking into consideration the amount to be paid, are much lower than life premiums. We know that a man must die, but a building may never burn down, therefore the risk is less.

COLLECTING

A man may insure in a dozen life insurance companies, and each must pay the amount of the policy on his death, but not so with fire companies.

A man owning a house worth, say ten thousand dollars, can insure it in ten companies, each taking a risk of eight thousand dollars.

If this house burns down the man does not receive eighty thousand dollars. The actual loss is calculated and the companies divide it up, each paying its part.

Fire companies, while anxious to issue policies on every insurable house, are more than willing that their business rivals should do the same, as in the event of fire the burden of loss will not be borne by one.

After every fire the company's agent examines the damage and estimates what is saved. On this the payment is based.

INSURABLE PROPERTY

A building is classed as real estate, but personal property is just as liable to be destroyed by fire.

Fire policies can be secured on goods, furniture, machinery, live stock and other things, and the method is about the same as where buildings are insured, but as a rule the premiums are higher, for such things are apt to be ruined by smoke and water, when the building in which they are stored may not be much injured.

MUTUAL COMPANIES

Men can associate for any legal purpose, and mutual protection against loss by fire is one of these.

In many neighborhoods throughout the country, but particularly in the eastern states, there are mutual insurance companies, usually composed of a number of men who know each other and who agree to share the losses of a member, in proportions agreed to in advance.

This form of insurance is cheap and effective, but the field of its operations is necessarily limited.

STOCK COMPANIES

The stock companies start with a fixed capital, each member receiving stock in proportion to the amount contributed.

The capital and the interest from it, after paying the necessary expenses, is invested, and reinvested, till it often reaches a large sum.

At the end of every fiscal year, usually June 30th, the expenses and the losses paid are deducted from the earnings and the net gain may be divided as dividends.

Often there are not only no dividends, but a great conflagration, like that of San Francisco, may wipe out all the earnings, all the reserve and even the capital itself, leaving the company bankrupt and heavily in debt.

Great calamities cannot be foreseen. No actuary has yet appeared to forecast the acts of Providence, but on the whole our fire insurance companies are well managed and prosperous.

ACCIDENT INSURANCE

We have insurance against storms, against the breaking of plate glass and even against loss from burglars, but the best known of the minor insurance societies are those known as "accident companies."

Accident policies are of many kinds, and there is no reason why the companies, under their charters, should not extend their risks indefinitely.

Accidents against property are insured much as is destruction from fire, but the nature of the accident as "hail," "explosions," "tornadoes" and "insect destruction" must be specified in the policy.

The most popular form of accident policy is that which is sold to travellers, and which can usually be had at the office where one buys his ticket.

The method here is simple, and the purchase may be made in a minute. "I want a policy for $1,000 for ten days," you say to the clerk. He tells you the amount, you pay and get your ticket, and there you are.

Prudent men have a stamped and addressed envelope ready. Into this they push the policy, and the wife gets it. No, it does not startle her. It is just Harry's prudence and she is used to that.

CHAPTER XXI

PARTNERSHIPS

If properly conducted, there is much to commend the management of a business through partners.

Never go into a partnership with a man who puts in his experience against your capital, unless you know him like a brother.

"It lasted about a year," said a man who had done this. "Now the fellow, who has cleared out, has the capital and I have the experience."

A partnership is an agreement between two or more persons to associate for the purpose of carrying on a certain form of business.

Each member of a copartnership must contribute a stated contribution to the establishment of the enterprise, but each need not give the same amount.

Neither is it necessary that the contributions of each to the firm shall be of the same character.

One may contribute a building, another machinery, or material, and still another money.

The shares in the profits are based on the cash values of the different contributions.

The work of the different parties may be estimated as contributions, but in such cases it is better to pay the worker a fixed compensation, and charge this to the expense account.

PREPARE AND SIGN

Never go into a partnership based on a verbal agreement, unless it be for the distribution of fish, game or nuts, when out with a friend for a holiday.

Have the copartnership articles carefully drawn up and signed before you put a cent into the undertaking. A document like this can be appealed to should disputes arise; and should a partner die, his heirs may find it of the greatest value.

The articles should contain:

1. The amount to be contributed by each. 2. The nature of the business. 3. The time which the partnership is to last.

If the time is not specified, a partner may withdraw whenever he pleases.

If the profits are to be equally divided, this should be stated and provided for.

SILENT PARTNERS

When a man invests money in a business in the management of which he takes no active part, he is said to be a "silent partner."

Such a partner has a share in the gains and he is responsible as the others for the firm's liabilities.

Again, a man may not give money or time to a firm, but is willing, for business reasons, that his name shall appear as if he were in the association. In this case the man is known as a "nominal partner."

Although this man is not entitled to a share in the profits and has no money invested, yet he can be held liable for the debts and other obligations. The reason for this is very plain.

LIABILITY

In all matters rightly belonging to the business of a firm, any member has the right to act, and his acts will be held binding in law.

It is usual for partners active in a business to have each his separate duties, but even if these duties be designated in the articles of agreement, the outside business world is not supposed to know anything about the relative duties of the members of a firm as decided among themselves, so it is decided that each is empowered to act for his partners.

Under the usual articles, it is stipulated that while a dual partnership lasts, neither of the members shall make a note, sign a bond, or enter on any outside obligation as an individual without having secured the written consent of his business associates.

Each partner in a firm is liable with the others for all the business indebtedness.

If a firm fails, and the assets are found not sufficient to satisfy the creditors, they can levy for satisfaction on the private property of one or all of the partners.

If a member of a firm should become so far indebted, as an individual, that he cannot comply with his obligations, the interest he holds in the firm may be disposed of and applied to the payment of his debts.

This does not mean that the creditors may take or seize on any particular thing which the firm holds jointly, but that the debtor's interest in the concern may be so disposed of. All this the law has provided for.

A new partner admitted into a firm cannot be held responsible for the debts of the old concern.

HOW TO DISSOLVE

Every partnership agreement must provide for and distinctly state the period for which it is to continue.

At the end of the period named, the partnership is dissolved by limitation.

If the partnership is to continue, a new agreement must be made and signed.

On proper application, a partnership may be dissolved by an order of the court.

If a member who has become objectionable to his partners should not agree to a dissolution of the firm, the partners may apply to a court of competent jurisdiction for a decree of dissolution.

No member of a firm can withdraw at his own option. The consent of the other partners is necessary, and before he is released he must provide for his share of the obligations.

Notice of dissolution should be published, and notices sent to agents and others interested.

The following is the customary form of notice:

The copartnership heretofore existing

between John Smith, Harry Roberts and

Thomas Allen, under the firm name of

Smith, Roberts & Co., is this day

dissolved by mutual consent.

John Smith.

Harry Roberts.

Thomas Allen.

June 30, 1910.

SPECIAL PARTNERSHIPS

Limited or special partners are not recognized in some states.

This is a method of association whereby a person joins a partnership, putting in a sum agreed on, and which he may stand to lose as an investment. He is entitled to a pro rata in the profits, but he cannot be held for the debts.

In some countries marriage is regarded as a civil contract or form of partnership, subject to dissolution by the courts.

CHAPTER XXII

INVESTMENTS

It is a remarkable fact that many men who have shown remarkable shrewdness in conducting a business in which a fortune may have been accumulated, exhibit the judgment of children when it comes to making investments.

There are able lawyers who have made fortunes in the practice of the profession which they understood, only to lose them by investments in mines or other ventures, about which they knew absolutely nothing but what was told them by the scheming speculator and smooth-tongued promoter.

As has been intimated before in these pages, there is a great difference between saving through and hoarding through a spirit of miserliness.

SAVINGS

Every wage or salary earner, no matter how small his compensation, should try to lay by something of that little as a provision against the unproductive days.

No matter how small the amount a man has set aside, after paying for life's necessities and meeting all just debts, he is to that extent a capitalist.

The miser would hide his savings out of reach, but the man with the foresight to save will usually have the judgment to place these savings where they will fructify and grow, producing the fruitage known as interest.

The young man or the young woman, or any one else who places his little accumulations in a savings bank, has begun a form of investment that may, if persisted in, place him or her above want, even if it does not entitle either to a place on the lists of great capitalists.

CAPITALISTS

The capitalist not only has money of his own to invest, but he may and very often does need more money properly to exploit the enterprises in which he is engaged.

Money loaned to such men, after being assured of their ability and integrity, is an advantage to the lender as it is to the user.

The lender's profit is assured if the enterprise does not fail, and the added capital not only insures against failure, but it may enable the manager to succeed beyond any expectations he could have if forced to carry on the work with only his own resources.

The capitalist may choose to buy land in the suburbs of a city and build thereon a house to be sold or rented. This should always be made to secure the money borrowed.

A capitalist may establish a fund from which, on good security, the business men of the community may obtain loans, for which they get a higher interest than that which they undertake to pay to those whose money they are using.

Again a capitalist may undertake to loan to farmers, who have not the means to carry on the work, but who are anxious to make their lands more productive, through drainage and crop rotation. In this case the money loaned is secured by the usual bond and mortgage.

Or it may be that another body of men is anxious to start a great manufacturing enterprise in the neighborhood, but has not enough money to place the venture on a paying basis.

In the latter case it appeals to the capitalist, and he, though not bearing enough available means of his own, undertakes the work with the knowledge that he can rely on the small investors, whose contributions he has before managed successfully.

STOCKHOLDERS

Or it may be that the manufacturing company does not ask the capitalist to assist, but itself goes to the small investor with a prospectus of the enterprise, and offers to sell stock in the concern at $50 or $100 a share, as the case may be.

This gives a chance to enjoy the profits, be they great or small; but with the chance for larger profits there comes the greater risk which must always be assumed in such cases.

Sometimes, when a company is starting, its stock may be put below par. This stock, in the event of success, may appreciate, as with some bank and other corporation stocks, many times above the par value.

When stocks sell in the open market for their face value, they are said to be at par.

KINDS OF STOCKS

Most companies, organized on a stock basis, issue stocks of two kinds. One is known as "common" the other as "preferred."

As the name implies, preferred stock (its rate of interest is always fixed) is entitled to be paid out of the net dividends first.

Whatever is left after paying the preferred stock interest is divided up equally among the shares of common stock, each getting according to his holdings.

Sometimes the dividends on common stock are far greater than those on the preferred. The preferred stock dividends are regarded as a fixed charge, but there can be no limit as to the payments on the common stock, if the funds are available.

The stocks of railroads, factories, banks and other enterprises may be good forms of investment, and for this they are often held for long periods by investors for revenue.

Most stocks, however, particularly of railroads, are continually changing hands. The buying and selling of such securities has grown to be an enormous business, managed largely by men known as "stock brokers," many of whom are strong factors in the financial world.

As a rule, the buying and selling of stocks through brokers is a hazardous form of speculation, which has in it all the elements of gambling, and we cannot advise too strongly against it.

There is another kind of stock, which some companies keep in their safes to meet an emergency. This is known as "treasury stock," and, like the preferred, its rate of interest is fixed.

Let us suppose that a company is capitalized and prints stock to the amount of $100,000.

This company sells $80,000 worth, and the officers believe that they can force the enterprise to success with the money on hand.

Now, it follows that, with the same amount of earnings, the profits on $80,000 will be greater than on $100,000, so the $20,000 unsold stock is held in reserve.

If to extend the business, or for any other reason, it is necessary to have more money, the treasury stock may be sold to secure the extra capital.

If the business is placed on a basis where its success is beyond all question, then the treasury stock may be divided pro rata between the holders of the other stock, for, till disposed of in some way, it was an asset common to the whole company.

Each stock certificate tells when dividends are declared; they may be paid quarterly, half yearly, or annually.

CHAPTER XXIII

BONDS AS INVESTMENTS

The best way in which savings can be invested is to use them in the extension of the business in which they were made.

The wage earner and the man on a salary cannot, of course, do this, but the farmer, the small tradesman, and the mechanic, who is his own employer, may be able to do so. And so, before looking for a field for investment outside, such men should look about them and consider how best the money may be used right on the ground.

AS TO BONDS

But after considering the points suggested, the man who has some money may not be able to find a secure and profitable place for it in or near his own home. One of the safest forms of investments is bonds, though, as with other forms of security, the rate of interest declines as the margin of safety increases.

If a well-established stock company should wish for any reason to increase its available cash, it may issue bonds, or certificate of indebtedness, bearing from four to five per cent interest, payable semi-annually.

These bonds may be transferred the same as stock. They are a good form of security when it is desired to borrow money from the bank, and for many purposes they are as available as so much cash.

Such bonds are issued for a specified number of years and have coupons attached, which are cut off when interest is due, and presented to the treasurer of the company for payment.

These bonds are secured by a mortgage or deed of trust on all the property of the corporation they represent.

To redeem these bonds, when due, the company annually sets apart a sum, known as a "Sinking fund," for their redemption.

Such bonds are far safer than any form of the company's stock, for they bear interest that must be met, whether or not dividends are declared.

As with a real estate mortgage, the property pledged in the bond should be defined.

RAILROAD BONDS

Every railroad in the country has been built and equipped by the sale of its bonds. In such cases amounts of stock of the same, or approximately the face value of the bond, have been given to the purchaser as a bonus or inducement. Of course, the controlling stock is always retained by the promoters; and it is through the representation of this stock that all the business of the corporation is carried on.

The cases are few where any money was paid directly for the original issue of any railroad stock.

Bonds sold to build a road are usually known as "construction" bonds. There may be another bond issue for equipment—with a stock bonus—and still other bonds, each series stating the property pledged and the purpose for which the money from sales is to be used.

The Christian Herald, in one of its recent financial articles, clearly defines this species of bonds, as follows:

"Railroad bonds are usually pledged by the President and Treasurer of the railroad and by the Trustees, to whom the bonds are made out, and who must defend the rights of bondholders, should the company fail to meet any of the obligations it undertook in the mortgage deed.

"In other words, a bond is the Corporation's promissory note for the money originally paid by the investor, with interest for the same, to be paid to the investor in stated amounts at stated intervals; and to guarantee its good faith in the matter, the Company pledges the bondholder an interest in certain property in its possession. It follows that a bond has a first call upon the property rights of the corporation; that it represents something tangible; that it pays a definite amount of interest, and that it may be reduced at its full value at a certain time."

BUYING BONDS

Bonds, like wheat, have their selling prices quoted from day to day, and they are equally a thing of purchase and sale.

There are banks and brokerage firms that make a specialty of bonds, and most of these houses are entirely reliable; still, the novice in such things would do well to investigate for himself before investing in any bond recommended by any seller.

It is the purpose of the seller to sell; it should be equally the purpose of the buyer not to be "sold."

Our government, state and municipal bonds speak for themselves, and in the main require no examination as to the security, though there have been cities and even states that have defaulted in their payments.

Bond houses and banks of established reputation cannot afford to deceive; they receive their compensation in the way of commissions on sales, and their characterization of the bonds may be accepted without question, for they invariably investigate the bonds, before they lend their names to them by offering them for sale.

If there is any doubt in the mind of the would be purchaser as to the character of the seller, that should be the first thing investigated.

What the buyer must satisfy himself of is:

1. Who is the seller? 2. What do the bonds represent? 3. Are they negotiable? and 4. Can they be sold again for about their face value?

Every one who has saved money, it is to be supposed, has a bank account and is acquainted with the president of his local bank. When in doubt, the advice of such a man may be of great help.

CHAPTER XXIV

THINGS TO REMEMBER

If a man is making a living he should not change his business after he has passed middle life, unless, indeed, he has a guarantee that the new venture will be greatly to his advantage.

The best business for the average man is that which affords him the most pleasure in carrying it on, or at least with which he is most familiar.

Happiness in one's work means far more than the accumulation of a fortune in discomfort.

DON'T DECEIVE YOURSELF

Having made your credit and business standing good, keep them good by an adherence to the same course.

If you can avoid it, do not loan your name to every needy friend that comes along. Your neighbors question your good judgment every time you have to meet a note which you were coaxed into endorsing. You would have saved yourself by loaning the money outright.

Do not deceive yourself into the belief that you are making money when, as a matter of fact, you may be losing.

You buy an article for two dollars and sell it for two and a half, and you say to yourself: "There is fifty cents made." But is it? Let us see.

Before crediting your business with that fifty cents, you should have considered these points.

1. The loss of interest on that two dollars. 2. Your own time or other time paid for. 3. The capital invested in things not sold. 4. The rent. 5. The transportation, insurance, heat, light, bad accounts, unsalable goods, taxes, public donations, and the flood of items that go to swell the outlay of every merchant, whether in the great city or at the country crossroads.

WEEDING OUT

Every man in trade should make an inventory of his stock at least once a year. Having done this, he should give his stock a fresh appearance, whether new goods be added or not, by relegating to the scrap heap, cellar or the garret all the dingy, dirty, disreputable stuff that he could not sell or give away, and which has induced sore eyes whenever seen.

Keep a stock book.

Quite as important as keeping the stock in order is keeping the books in good shape.

At least once a year the books should be weeded out. Why carry as bills collectable accounts which you have been assured, for years, would never be paid?

Wipe them out and charge them to profit and loss.

Where machinery is used, it is a good plan to charge off every year ten per cent of the cost; this to make good the loss from wear and tear.

It is only by annual house cleanings and account clearings that you can tell about how you stand.

LET YOUR WIFE KNOW

It is usually wise for a woman, married or single, to keep her real estate and her money, if she have any, in her own name. So also with property bought with her money.

In these cases the woman should deal with her husband, or the members of her family, the same as she would with strangers with whom she is transacting business.

Some may say that this suggests a want of confidence and a lack of that affection that should exist between husband and wife or near kinsfolk. Such an objection is sheer sentimentality. Be as open handed and generous as you will with your loved ones, but when it comes to business, let the work be done in a strictly business way or not at all.

Many a good business has gone to ruin after the death of the owner and manager because he had kept his wife in blank ignorance of his affairs and the way in which he conducted them.

Many a business, that just dragged along till the death of the manager, has sprung into new life when the widow took charge. This must in part be credited to natural ability and inborn pluck and energy, but even these gifts could not have availed if the woman had been left in ignorance of business methods.

Women, like men, are awkward in new positions, not so much from a want of ability as a lack of experience.

Put the average man suddenly in charge of a house, and he will soon demonstrate his helplessness. The woman's deftness comes from her experience.

As far as it is possible, every husband should post his wife as to his methods of doing business.

He should not keep her ignorant of his financial affairs.

If he conceal from her the amount of his secure holdings, it may be that he hopes to surprise her at his death, or long before that event. But if he have any regard for his family, he should not hide from her the obligations which may spell ruin if the wife is not prepared in advance to meet them.

Whether the husband lives or dies, the wife must still care for the children and attend to her never-lessening household duties. Think of her as taking on the added burdens of a business of which she is ignorant.

There are many prosperous husbands to whom what has just been said will not apply, but if you should ask them the secret of their success they will not hesitate to tell you that when they married they took their wives into full partnership, business secrets and all.

CHILDREN AND BUSINESS

When you send your children to school it is that the training there received may qualify them to fight the better the ceaseless life battle.

Of course, we should not regard all education from a business viewpoint. Money apart, learning is its own greatest reward.

It widens the horizon at every step, and lifts the soul into strength and a profounder worship. But it will not do to overlook the business side of the training which the child should receive in school and out of it.

It is all very well to teach children the sources of the family revenue and the way to secure it. It is right that they should be impressed with the dignity of labor and trained in the ways of earning money, but it is far more important that they should be taught how to spend money, so as to get the most good from it, once it is earned.

The boy or girl is in a safe way to learn self-control and build up character when he or she, with some nickels at command, can pass a candy or a fruit shop without being compelled to spend their cash assets.

Children, wherever it is possible, should be given opportunities for earning money, which they can feel is "really and truly" their own.

They should not be made to feel that the money is not actually theirs, to do with as they please, but they should be taught self- denial, and that they must not get rid of their earnings by the purchase of things not needed.

On the farm, children unconsciously learn much through occasional work and constant observation, but away from the farm, boys and girls are apt to know little or nothing of the work in which the father, the bread winner, is engaged.

Where it is possible, the children should be made familiar by actual contact with the father's work.

This knowledge may never be used, still it will have value as a factor in the child's training, for in our modern life all business is inter-related.

Let the youngsters know something about banks by entrusting them there when old enough.

Teach them to keep accounts of their own little money affairs, their earnings, their expenditures, and their balances.

If they should borrow, even a cent, see that they return it at the time agreed on. Impress on them the fact that debt is a burden which it is well to get rid of as soon as possible, if one would stand erect and be entirely free.

All this can be quietly inculcated into the mind of the child without making him old-fashioned or miserly. The more he knows of the world the more he can enjoy it in a wholesome way.